Dyslexia-Friendly Further & Higher Education

Dyslexia-Friendly
Further & Higher
Education

Barbara Pavey
Margaret Meehan
Alan Waugh

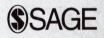

SSAGE

Los Angeles | London | New Delhi
Singapore | Washington DC

First published 2010

SAGE Publications Ltd
1 Oliver's Yard
55 City Road
London EC1Y 1SP

SAGE Publications Inc.
2455 Teller Road
Thousand Oaks, California 91320

SAGE Publications India Pvt Ltd
B 1/I 1 Mohan Cooperative Industrial Area
Mathura Road
New Delhi 110 044

SAGE Publications Asia-Pacific Pte Ltd
33 Pekin Street #02-01
Far East Square
Singapore 048763

Library of Congress Control Number: 2009928863

British Library Cataloguing in Publication data

A catalogue record for this book is available from the British Library

ISBN 978-1-84787-585-3
ISBN 978-1-84787-586-0 (pbk)

Typeset by C&M Digitals (P) Ltd, Chennai, India
Printed in Great Britain by Biddles Ltd, King's Lyn
Printed on paper from sustainable resources

Mixed Sources
Product group from well-managed forests and other controlled sources
www.fsc.org Cert no. SA-COC-1565
© 1996 Forest Stewardship Council
FSC

This book is dedicated to Peter Pumfrey

Contents

9   Dyslexia and disability-friendly perspectives   87
Barbara Pavey, Margaret Meehan and Alan Waugh

Appendices   97

Acknowledgements

The authors would like to thank Jane Stroud, Neil Gilbride, Robert Edwards, Sandy Cross, Christine McCall and others who have read extracts for us or discussed with us the points raised. We would also like to thank Orla ni Dhubhghaill, Trevor Spalding, Mary O'Grady, Janet Thomas and Alison Doyle for advice about Ireland; Marie Maunsell-Stuart for advice about 14+ provision in FE, and Professor Angela Fawcett of Swansea University for advice about the ISHEDS project.

We would like to acknowledge that the audit tool (Appendix 2) and the lesson/lecture plan in Appendix 6 follow similar items, but have been amended for FE and HE, to those developed in Pavey (2007). The essay-writing template and word count guidelines (Appendix 5) appear in Martin and Pavey (2008) and are published here with the permission of the University of Birmingham.

We are grateful to Naomi Garrett of Widgit Software, for providing us with the image at the start of Chapter 5. We would like also to thank Jude Bowen, Amy Jarrold and colleagues at Sage Publishing and Deer Park Productions.

Finally, we would like to thank our students, and also our colleagues in FE and HE who experience dyslexia in their own right, and whose experience and insight inform this book.

About the authors

Barbara Pavey   has been an inclusion and special education practitioner in a range of settings, including primary, secondary, specialist, FE and HE. She has been a SENCO and a local authority educational officer in SEN, and holds a rights-based view of education, focusing on helping practitioners to enable pupils and students to make progress. She is a senior lecturer in the Faculty of Education and Theology at York St John University.

Margaret Meehan   has worked with adults with specific learning difficulties in HE for over 15 years. Initially working with dyslexic students who experienced difficulties with mathematics and science, Margaret subsequently worked with students across all disciplines. Her training in advanced counselling skills enables Margaret to understand how specific learning difficulties impinge on every aspect of daily living.

Alan Waugh   has been involved with post-16 education for 12 years and has always worked with learners who have experienced specific learning difficulties, including dyslexia, dyspraxia and autistic spectrum disorder. Currently Programme Area Manager for Learner Support at City College, Coventry, Alan works with a diverse range of learners and he advises colleagues in the curriculum areas.

Introduction

Who is this book for?

Whether or not concepts and theories of dyslexia are challenged by critics, it remains important to meet the learning needs of students in further and higher education (FE and HE respectively). This requirement extends beyond the domain of specialist support; it is a responsibility for all members of staff in all institutions. The challenges set by the government mean that there will be more learners being identified as experiencing dyslexia. This book is written not only for educators who are already knowledgeable in this area but also for regular practitioners who want to understand more about dyslexia in order to improve their practice, to help their students to achieve satisfactory outcomes, and to make sure that students' expectations, requirements and rights are met.

There has been a number of items of legislation, Codes of Practice and sets of standards governing the expansion of further and higher education to include learners with disabilities and/or difficulties. One significant Code that is considered throughout this book is the Disability Rights Commission revised *Code of Practice for Post-16 Education* (DRC, 2007). Other Codes also give important guidance, such as the Quality Assurance Agency's *Code of Practice for the Assurance of Academic Quality and Standards in Higher Education, Section 3: Students with Disabilities* (QAA, 1999), which is currently under revision, (QAA, 2009), and the Department for Education and Skills' *Special Educational Needs Code of Practice* (DfES, 2001). Of considerable importance also is the Code of Practice resulting from the 2005 amendment to the Disability Discrimination Act, *The Duty to Promote Equality of Opportunity* (DRC, 2005). Together these provide necessary guidance for current UK practice.

We argue that the best way of meeting the duties for students who experience dyslexia, including the anticipatory duty, the duty to make advantageous arrangements and the duty to promote equality of opportunity, is to adopt a dyslexia-friendly perspective, not only among specialists but also among all members of staff in FE and HE. Such an approach ideally would include attention to administrative as well as pedagogic processes.

The trajectory of this book moves from the social to the psychological perspective in dyslexia discourse. However, the direct focus of this book is upon dyslexia-friendly teaching and learning in FE and HE. Its purpose is to offer a text that will support relevant inclusion and specialist study, but also to offer guidance and activity that will inform mainstream, academic-related programmes and in-service training.

Defining dyslexia

There are very many different definitions of dyslexia. Educators continue to seek the precise wording to describe their particular understanding of dyslexia, whether it is perceived as a difficulty, disability or disorder. For the purpose of this book the British Dyslexia Association's (BDA) definition, available at www.bdadyslexia.org.uk, is considered to offer a standard. It is probably the most frequently used and most easily reached by interested parties. The BDA states that:

> Dyslexia is a specific learning difficulty that mainly affects the development of literacy and language related skills. It is likely to be present at birth and life-long in its effects. It is characterised by difficulties with phonological processing, rapid naming, working memory processing speed and the automatic development of skills that may not match up to an individual's other cognitive abilities. It tends to be resistant to conventional teaching methods, but its effects can be mitigated by appropriately specific intervention, including the application of information technology and supportive counselling (Singleton, 2008).

 This portmanteau definition embodies the current understanding of dyslexia, from a psychological, individual deficit view. However, viewed from the perspective of the social model of disability, Ross Cooper's 2006 summation may be preferred:

> We would argue that dyslexia is an experience that arises out of natural human diversity on the one hand and a world on the other where the early learning of literacy, and good personal organisation and working memory is mistakenly used as a marker of 'intelligence'. The problem here is seeing difference incorrectly as 'deficit' (Cooper, 2006: 24).

How to use this book

This book is structured to cater to readers' diverse needs. It acts both as a textbook and as a resource for non-specialists. Each chapter includes a discursive section, followed by relevant features informing pedagogy and practice. In addition to being read in their conventional themed format, the chapters can also be read across their explanatory sections or across their features. Finally, the appendices provide tools to support dyslexia-friendly practice.

Each chapter opens with an overview expressed in graphical terms, using software that is available to students receiving dyslexia support in FE and HE, and concludes with a summary of three key points and a student's view. Each chapter contains an exploration of its main theme and a key technique that can be used by non-specialists to support dyslexia-friendly teaching and learning, plus a focus on current debate.

Following this, the chapters contain guidance from the 2007 DDA Code of Practice and a case study. Specialist tutors in FE and HE provide advice, linking their specialist knowledge of dyslexia with real examples drawn from non-specialist experience. The case studies can be used for enquiry-based learning. Suitable questions are provided to stimulate discussion and the actual outcomes are described. The chapters close with a summary and suggestions for further reading, along with details for accessing the software illustrated at the start of the chapter.

1

Dyslexia and the implications for 14–19 and adult learning

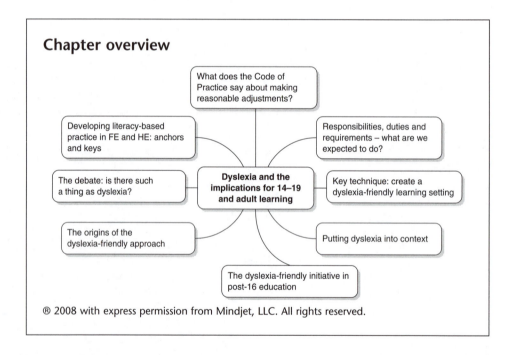

Chapter overview

- What does the Code of Practice say about making reasonable adjustments?
- Developing literacy-based practice in FE and HE: anchors and keys
- Responsibilities, duties and requirements – what are we expected to do?
- The debate: is there such a thing as dyslexia?
- **Dyslexia and the implications for 14–19 and adult learning**
- Key technique: create a dyslexia-friendly learning setting
- The origins of the dyslexia-friendly approach
- Putting dyslexia into context
- The dyslexia-friendly initiative in post-16 education

Responsibilities, duties and requirements – what are we expected to do?

The provision of a state education system is an act of social engineering based on social and political beliefs that the intervention offered therein will improve quality of life, both for individuals and for society as a whole. Underpinning this is a conception of society which may or may not be questioned by educators themselves. Currently, educational function in the UK is focused on the targets of developing expertise in STEM subjects (science, technology, engineering and mathematics) and on employability and entrepreneurship, supporting a vision of an economy based upon the generation and development of ideas and knowledge.

Policies and guidance underpin this movement, promoting lifelong learning and widening participation. For learners with difficulties and/or disabilities, the world of education has duties to provide access and to promote equality of opportunity. Included within these are the duty to make special adjustments and the duty not to treat disabled people less favourably, even to the point of treating learners with disabilities and difficulties more favourably (DRC, 2005: 23).

In the UK, the 2001 SEN and Disability Act amended the Disability Discrimination Act of 1995, becoming Part IV of that Act, thereby extending the DDA 1995 to include provisions for education. A further statutory instrument, which carries the same legal obligation as the Act itself, brought in regulations for further and higher education in 2006. These legislativ provisions bring the UK in line with the European Employment Framework Directive (DRC, 2007: iv), contributing to a suite of initiatives, policies and legislative actions, intended to lead towards employability and employment for a wider population. Added to this is the continuing importance of literacy; accordingly dyslexia has gained an increasingly higher profile.

The trend towards a changing population in FE and HE is not without resistance. It may therefore come as a surprise to some that legislation and policy have firmly settled on the side of learners with difficulties and/or disabilities. For many people, when, or if, they think about disability, it is with a view to treating students 'fairly'. However, this is not only incorrect, it is dangerous for institutions.

From time to time the popular media may carry accusations of unfairness when adjustments are made to take account of disability, especially in the case of dyslexia. This is particularly so when the argument is directed against learners who seem to be unfairly advantaged, perhaps because their dyslexia is towards the milder end of the range, as is frequently the case in HE. This is because the concepts of social justice, upon which reasonable adjustments are based, are not widely understood. These concepts are founded upon earlier ideas about the politics of recognition and the politics of distribution. The origins of these may be attributed to Rawls' work in considering justice through distribution (first principle) and then advantageous redistribution (second principle) in *A Theory of Justice* (Rawls, 1971), to Taylor's work ('The politics of recognition' 1974) and to Honneth's work on the concept of justice through recognition, which could itself include redistribution (see for example Honneth, 2004). These concepts focus on how goods and resources are distributed throughout society in order to ensure more equitable treatment. They may include ideas about 'fair shares', 'level playing fields' and the redistribution of resources through policies and taxes. These ideas do not necessarily trouble existing locations of power and resources. However, the recognition concept goes further, it includes identity politics, and is expressed here through the perspective of making special arrangements and particular adjustments in favour of disadvantaged people; in this case, people experiencing dyslexia.

There should be no doubt that present-day policy, practice and legislation are oriented around the politics of recognition. Anything else operates against disadvantaged groups and individuals; fair shares are not fair when one sector of the population is disadvantaged already. However, there are other challenges of unfairness in the popular perception of dyslexia. These come from the continuing scepticism that surrounds dyslexia, which has its origins in the lack of certainty about what dyslexia is, or might be, how we understand and describe it and how we assess it.

Putting dyslexia into context

The understanding of dyslexia continues to develop and evolve, yet the dyslexia debate continues, with no definition currently in existence that completely satisfies all interested parties. This is partly as a result of the different discourses within dyslexia, both psychological and sociological, and partly because there is, as yet, no complete agreement as to the nature of dyslexia. Denials of dyslexia generally turn out to be challenges to the way dyslexia is discussed or assessed. In consequence, there is no guarantee that discussions about dyslexia are considering the same factors. Contributing to this disparity is the fact that there are views of dyslexia that consider it to be a cause, while others see it as an effect.

A fundamental issue in dyslexia remains that of whether dyslexia is a separate entity, a characteristic that exists in some learners and not in others, or whether it is the expression of the extreme end of the range of difficulty in acquisition of literacy skills. The latter argument might merge with the former by considering whether there may be a point in this range where the difficulty becomes so extreme that it can be identified as a characteristic in its own right. However, this view would need to be explored further.

A further key issue is the point that conceptualisations of dyslexia are so wide and varied that they seem not to be describing one particular phenomenon. Consequently for some, 'dyslexia' might now be understood as an umbrella term, while others focus upon subtypes (about which there is also a lack of strong agreement) or upon consideration of whether the main dyslexia theories can be reconciled.

Regardless of the conceptualisation of dyslexia, there is no doubt that for some people, the skills of literacy acquisition are very difficult, to the extent that they may consider themselves, or be considered by others, as illiterate. It is also clear that this difficulty is particularly resistant to standard teaching and learning for literacy, but may also be both unusual and striking in terms of other skills and potential for learning that a person might have. Discussions continue as to whether other characteristics, such as creativity or practical ability, are associated with dyslexia in any firm way.

 Whether it is conceptualised as a disability, difficulty or difference, dyslexia is a hidden characteristic, and the time and effort spent on checking, double-checking and correcting by people who experience dyslexia is not noticed by others and therefore not respected or understood. Further, the support now available to dyslexic learners in FE and HE may be viewed simplistically as compensating for dyslexia, so that it effectively disappears. This is not the case. Dyslexia continues, and while many learners overcome their difficulties brilliantly, this still requires time, effort and practice, and causes additional fatigue.

The education system attempts to provide a safety net, recognising the increasing importance of literacy in the modern world. In addition, a reconsideration of the developmental process of learning as embodied in the Lifelong Learning initiative now supports the view that it is never too late to learn. So, while it is unlikely that a person with severely reduced literacy skills will be studying in HE, there may be students whose higher level literacy skills were acquired later in their lives, and who have taken advantage of Access programmes. Additionally, FE colleges and independent providers of work-based training may find, within their intake, learners with only a rudimentary level of literacy. For some students their literacy difficulty is likely to be the result of unidentified dyslexia.

The origins of the dyslexia-friendly approach

The British Dyslexia Association's (BDA) dyslexia-friendly initiative in local authorities and schools, launched in 1999, received a positive response. Five years later, it was followed by a quality mark process aimed at local authorities. The dyslexia-friendly approach did more than move the focus of provision into schools; it included the environmental aspects of the learning setting, by seeking to make learning more accessible to children and young people experiencing dyslexia. It also caught the mood of the ethical and philosophical change that was pervading education through increasing awareness of the social rights model of disability. The social model supports the view that while an individual may experience impairments, it is the social situation, both practical and attitudinal, that is disabling.

The dyslexia-friendly approach does not take an individual-deficit focus, and this may present some difficulties to people who prefer such a view. The dyslexia-friendly approach places the emphasis upon creating a learning setting, from the top down, that is sensitive to the learning requirements in dyslexia. It includes the belief that effective teaching for learners with dyslexia is effective teaching for all learners with special educational needs, learning difficulties and/or disabilities. Much of the initiative is concerned with creating a supporting ethos with an inbuilt expectation that this will develop and grow, pervading the whole learning setting. This expectation extends to elements in the infrastructure, including those within local authority policy and practice.

The dyslexia-friendly initiative in post-16 education

The dyslexia-friendly approach expects that what is good for dyslexic learners is good for all learners. The possibility of gaining the BDA's dyslexia-friendly quality mark has now been extended to FE colleges and college departments, and to independent trainers and providers, transferring dyslexia-friendly principles to the post-16 setting. The mission statement for FE is:

To promote excellent practice by the college as it carries out its role of supporting and challenging its staff to improve accessibility for more learners. (BDA, n.d.)

For practitioners this includes sharing good practice and encouraging colleagues to review their practice in the classroom. This removes inherent barriers to learning and thereby increases the opportunities for learners with specific learning difficulties, including dyslexia, to achieve their educational goals.

The FE and training provider protocols are very similar. As with the LA Quality Mark process, the institution or department assesses its dyslexia-friendly characteristics against four categories: focusing, developing, established and enhancing. The process is comprehensive, addressing pre-determined standards in the following five areas:

- the effectiveness of the management structure
- the identification of dyslexia/SpLD
- the effectiveness of resources (physical environment, teaching and learning)
- continuing professional development
- partnership with learners, parents or carers and external agencies.

These are matched against the development criteria. Guidance from the BDA clarifies these, confirming that the meaning of 'focusing' is that an area requiring further development has been identified; 'developing' indicates that work in the relevant area is progressing; 'established' means that identified dyslexia-friendly processes are taking place as standard; and 'enhancing' means that practice that is taking place beyond the level required by the standard.

Like other quality mark procedures, assessment is carried out by a self-audit, supported by documentary evidence. This is scrutinised by verifiers and the paper evidence is augmented by interviews and discussion. As with the LA and school Quality Mark processes, the aim is to raise the standard of dyslexia awareness and practice, and to embed it throughout colleges and training establishments, rather than consigning it solely to the province of specialists.

Developing literacy-based practice in FE and HE: anchors and keys

For professionals in FE and HE trying to negotiate the territory of reasonable adjustment, fair treatment and the demands of marking criteria in dealing with the written work of students who may experience dyslexia, it is useful to know the points at which discussion no longer applies. These points are 'givens' and are incontrovertible (or nearly so), thus they are described here as 'anchors':

1 The politics of recognition, giving rise to legislation and policy expressed in the duty to anticipate the need for reasonable adjustments.

2 The descriptors of scholarship and academic attainments that form the QAA's academic framework (QAA, 2001; 2008) and that are given expression via institutions' marking criteria.
3 Rights under the Disability Discrimination Act, as amended by the Special Educational Needs and Disability Act (SENDA) 2001 and revised in 2005. These rights apply to all students studying within the UK, whatever their country of origin.
4 Codes of Practice and practice guides, especially those of QAA, DRC, and SEN, plus the dyslexia policies predicated upon these.
5 Students' learning support agreements, or individual learning plans, which indicate what professionals should do to meet students' learning needs.

Knowledge about these anchors and of what they consist, can and should be applied to professional work in FE and HE to ensure dyslexia-friendly practice in written work and in all scholastic tasks. The following 'keys' to dyslexia-friendly practice clarify how these principles may be applied.

In assessment tasks we can:

- present assessment tasks so that they are easy to read and follow
- avoid switching modes during the assessment. This means avoiding a change in the style of the answer, or a change such as moving from looking for features that are alike, to looking for features that are different, without warning the reader
- vary the methods of assessment (e.g. by using portfolios, presentations, posters, etc.)
- arrange assessment feedback so that students know how to make progress. (e.g. by target setting.)

In an assignment, tutorial or seminar we can:

- graphically organise the assignment for an individual, group or class, converting it to a list if some find that easier to follow
- ask students to verbalise their assignment ideas; we can then graphically organise or otherwise record what they say as discussion progresses (preferably on tinted card), then give them the notes of their own words to take away
- avoid assuming that starting points or key points are the same for the tutor and the student; linear thought may have less relevance or clarity for a dyslexic student than for the tutor leading the discussion.

In teaching and lecturing we can:

- use multisensory methods
- 'chunk' the tasks
- give the 'big picture' before linear progression

- take care with font size and style
- arrange text in small blocks and place these near relevant pictures or diagrams
- allow extra time
- use and offer tinted paper as standard
- give handouts in advance
- avoid setting long copying tasks
- avoid expecting students to take copious notes
- find ways of teaching that do not depend on pencil and paper tasks
- look for quality rather than quantity.

The debate: is there such a thing as dyslexia?

Arguments continue as to whether there is or is not such a thing as dyslexia. Debate is framed around the lack of agreed understanding about what does or does not constitute its characteristics, and how these many be identified. Challenges are made on the basis of descriptors being too wide and vague, or the means of assessment being compromised by bias or weakness, or the lack of an agreed definition, which may be seen as proof that no single character-istic called 'dyslexia' can be said to exist.

In contrast, policies and preferences that do not use the term 'dyslexia' may be denounced as avoidances, pretences and excuses for not helping learners. Such policies may actually be based on decisions not to use a term that seems ambiguous, or on a wish to focus upon providing help rather than a label, or on a resource model that seeks to support learners in accordance with their level of need. The debate continues in spite of government willingness to use the term 'dyslexia' and recognise its existence as a discrete condition.

Key technique: create a dyslexia-friendly learning setting

In FE and HE, a room or venue is not 'owned' by a practitioner in the same way as is a classroom in a school. Some rooms may become accustomed territory when they are regularly used and others are purpose built for specific study. Good practice suggests that learning and study environments should be dyslexia-friendly, and minimise the barriers to learning that can, inadvertently, be put in place. The departmental self-evaluation/audit tool in Appendix 2 provides a checklist to enable practitioners to do this. It includes sections on text resources available in the classroom, study room or lecture theatre; room arrangements; affective aspects; room interactions; and gen-eral teaching and learning for good dyslexia-friendly practice. The audit tool can be used on an individual level, but as a dyslexia-friendly principle, the process should be used by all, and has therefore been framed around depart-mental or group practice.

What does the Code of Practice say about making reasonable adjustments?

All the Codes support the need to make adjustments for students with difficulties and/or disabilities such as dyslexia. *The Disability Discrimination Act 1995: Code of Practice Post-16* (DRC, 2007) devotes much of its content to this matter. It points out that the duty to anticipate the need to make reasonable adjustments for disabled students is not just focused upon study but extends to all aspects of the educational experience. This includes relationships when someone is no longer a student at the institution, such as when they are invited back to a post-graduation event (DRC, 2007; para. 9.51).

 ## Case study: Mike; who tutors the tutor?

Dyslexia-friendly FE and HE are not only about supporting students; staff may also experience dyslexia. Mike, aged 42, was working as a support tutor when the head of his department asked him to raise the level of his dyslexia qualification through part-time study, telling him that the institution was willing to cover the fee. As a person who experienced dyslexia himself, Mike, in his role as student, underwent a needs assessment and gained support from his local authority in the form of a computer and software, and a book allowance. However, he found himself in a difficult position when it came to the kind of support that he himself would have given his students. There was no one to talk to about his studies, or to ask for advice, or to help him to improve his written expression. Some techniques he knew from his own work, but he found it hard to apply these to his own studies.

The FE dyslexia specialist comments

There should have been the provision in place for tutor support as part of the needs assessment to be funded by the local authority (LA). The institution should support Mike by helping him to find a private tutor; after all, this is professional development for the benefit of the employers and its 'customers', who are the students. Course teaching teams could provide additional tutorials to ensure understanding of assignments and course topics.

The HE dyslexia specialist comments

If the needs assessor has judged that Mike needs specialist tuition and the local authority has approved this, Mike could then contact the LA and ask if he could find his own specialist tutor and the tutor could bill the LA directly. This would give Mike the freedom to choose an appropriate tutor, perhaps from the Association of Dyslexia Specialists in Higher Education (ADSHE) forum.

〰〰 Points for discussion

- Is the request from Mike's head of department a reasonable one?
- Whose responsibility is it to support Mike in his studies?
- As a professional working in the field of dyslexia, should Mike be able to manage his own study needs?
- Should Mike remind his programme tutors occasionally about his dyslexia?

The outcome was that Mike continued to manage his studies on his own. A learning support agreement for him was on file, but there is no knowing whether all his tutors had seen it, or having seen it, remembered its provisions. His head of department believed that Mike had access to everything he needed and could supplement assistive technology with his own professional knowledge. For Mike the experience of this higher level study was arduous, time consuming and fatiguing. He needed the full amount of time available to him to complete the course and the experience was challenging, but ultimately he achieved his higher level qualification.

▢ Summary

1 Widening participation, Access, and Lifelong Learning policies, together with national drives to increase literacy, mean that more young people with identified difficulties and disabilities, and more adults of all ages, are entering FE and HE. A proportion of new students will be identified as experiencing dyslexia, either before or during their studies.
2 Duties reside in legislation, regulation and policy, and are based upon a perception of justice through recognition. These duties are clarified in the relevant Codes of Practice. They place responsibilities on all practitioners, not just to respond to student's learning needs, but to anticipate them, even to the point of making advantageous arrangements.
3 Debate continues, both about the nature of dyslexia and about the existence of dyslexia as a separate characteristic. Nevertheless, regardless of debate or opinion, there are duties for professionals in FE and HE to support learners identified with dyslexia.

Further reading 📖

Department for Education and Skills (DfES) (2004) *A Framework for Understanding Dyslexia*. Annesley: DfES Publications.

Pollak, D. (2005) *Dyslexia, the Self, and Higher Education*. Stoke on Trent: Trentham Books.

Reid, G., Fawcett, A., Manis, F. and Seigel, L. (eds) (2008) *The Sage Handbook of Dyslexia*. London: Sage.

Assistive software

The graphical representation at the start of this chapter is constructed with Mindjet software. This is one of several alternative packages available to aid the graphic organisation of work and could be used by practitioners and students alike. Mindjet is available from: www.mindjet.com/en-GB

Student comment

'With one-to-one tuition you [the student] can set the agenda, work through a series of issues, and plan your work ahead. I think where individual help can be given, you're better for it because it's an invaluable tool'. Bernadette

2

The dyslexia-friendly college

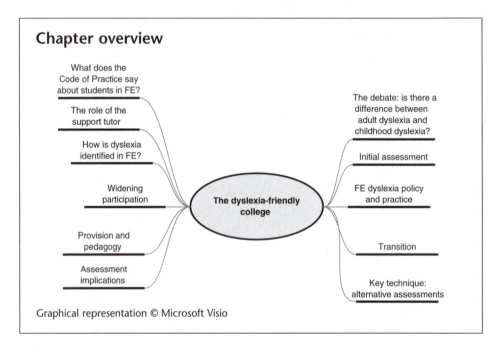

Chapter overview

What does the Code of Practice say about students in FE?

The role of the support tutor

How is dyslexia identified in FE?

Widening participation

Provision and pedagogy

Assessment implications

The dyslexia-friendly college

The debate: is there a difference between adult dyslexia and childhood dyslexia?

Initial assessment

FE dyslexia policy and practice

Transition

Key technique: alternative assessments

Graphical representation © Microsoft Visio

FE dyslexia policy and practice

Post-16 education is going through a phase of repositioning in order to meet the needs of the community to ensure that a skilled workforce is equipped to compete in the global market. The sector now includes FE colleges, community colleges and tertiary colleges. In addition, some colleges offer higher educational provision. There are other FE contexts such as specialist colleges, prison contracts, armed forces, FE within the school setting, independent training providers, and adult and community-based education.

The range and nature of post-16 qualifications are also changing to meet the requirements of the modern workplace. The Leitch review (Leitch, 2006) has set the target of 95 per cent of adults who will have the basic skills of functional literacy and numeracy by 2020, and it is expected that in excess of 90 per cent of adults will have achieved a minimum of a Level 2 qualification. To maximise learning opportunities, all colleges need a policy that covers the identification, assessment and support of learners. A model for such a policy is shown in Appendix 3.

A college prospectus will need to describe the provision made for students who may experience dyslexia or other learning characteristics. A key indicator for Ofsted inspectors is the date when a student was identified as requiring support compared with when the support was put in place. The importance of this is that a learner may be struggling unnecessarily and leave the course feeling that their abilities were inadequate, when all that was required was support and an assessment of their needs to be more timely.

It is possible that nowadays there is generally more awareness among teaching teams who are able to recognise the indicators that a learner may be struggling, possibly because of dyslexia. All staff should be aware of the referral process if a learner has not already been identified at the initial assessment stage. Dyslexia awareness and professional development sessions for staff should be an ongoing part of staff training days as well as being encompassed in the units of the teacher training qualifications. Staff may need to be reminded of legislation and policy requirements in order to maintain a dyslexia-friendly ethos, and their first priority should be to make the content of the lesson accessible.

Widening participation

An Ofsted inspection will consider how well colleges meet targets for educational and social inclusion. Inspectors will look at how much effort is made to increase access to further education and training, particularly for students who are difficult to engage. Bringing about such engagement will require a broad range of teaching and training skills to be able to include the varied educational abilities needed to achieve a successful outcome. This may mean that the delivery of some provision will be external from the college, for instance in community centres.

A consideration of the support needs of all learners may also include personal and welfare support. It is intended that young people from disadvantaged backgrounds should take the opportunity of improving their skills and employability options. Further support is available for dyslexic students, as it is for others experiencing disadvantage, through the Adult Learning Grant, introduced as a way of increasing the participation in Level 3 courses for those aged 19–25.

Initiatives will be judged on retention and achievement targets, with a focus on the development of literacy, numeracy and language skills. It is more motivating to judge the 'distance travelled' by some learners in terms of their personal development and learning goals achieved. An example may be a project that works with young offenders developing their basic skills and personal skills. The act of engaging in education after a negative earlier experience in childhood is a major step for some, particularly older adults. The thought of experiencing an examination and possible failure, or external pressures that produce barriers to learning, are obstacles that can be overcome only by time and patience.

Access to higher education courses are run in collaboration with an HE institution. These courses will attract adults who are keen to re-train or improve their employment prospects. Learners on Access courses may require a specialist learning assessment. This is important to ensure that an application can be made for Disabled Students' Allowance (DSA) when progressing to university and to ensure proper access arrangements are in place.

Provision and pedagogy

The majority of teaching staff in further education and independent training provision have come from a previous industrial and vocational background, bringing with them a wealth of knowledge and experience in their field of expertise. They will have to learn how to become part of a new profession – that of teacher, tutor and lecturer. New skills and knowledge will have to be taken on board to manage the classroom and workshop areas as well as learning the theory of teaching practice. There will be occasions when a specialist teacher in college will be working with colleagues who have found that they are struggling themselves with literacy elements; an assessment may show that they are experiencing a specific learning difficulty. This should be seen as setting a positive example for the college, since it enables learners to see that a career path is achievable.

The *Leitch Review of Skills* has led to the requirement for all teaching staff in FE to achieve the revised qualifications that will have replaced the Certificate of Education by the year 2010, leading to a licensed practitioner status and registration with the Institute for Learning. This professional body will be responsible for ensuring the continuous professional development of all teaching staff in the post-16 education sector. Teaching methodology has developed to focus on personalised learning and the learning style of individual learners. This has its advantages when dealing with dyslexic learners. Teaching staff will be advised by the specialist teacher in the college, and strategies that support a dyslexic learner in class will benefit all learners.

Transition

Transition planning for learners is crucial for effective allocation of resources and for ensuring appropriate support is put in place. Whether or not there is a formal transition plan, close links with schools and their special educational needs coordinators (SENCOs) are essential for sharing information, with learners' permission. This allows for the opportunity to talk to young people about their support, whether they have felt that one-to-one support was beneficial, or whether they have a preference for in-class support or small group work. Many will comment that they did not like being sent out of the middle of a lesson to attend their support session and that they felt 'singled out' by in-class support.

In post-16 education there is a greater opportunity to negotiate alternative days and times for support input as students are not attending lessons for the same amount of time as they would during a normal school week. In addition to specialist support, it may be necessary to provide a note-taker in class or negotiate the use of a voice recorder in lessons with colleagues on the teaching team. In a vocational class, such as construction or engineering, it would not be unusual for a number of learners to require support in the class; the practical aspect of these areas may attract dyslexic learners who exhibit good practical skills.

How is dyslexia identified in FE?

Diagnostic assessments can be carried out only by a specialist teacher or an educational psychologist, but learners should be supported for their course of study at the earliest opportunity, so an interview for the course will also be a means of identification. New applicants are invited to tick a box on college course application forms indicating if they experience a disability or if support is required in literacy or numeracy. It is more common now for course tutors to ask prospective students whether they have experienced difficulties or received support at school. When parents accompany their children to the interview they will often raise issues that were a concern at school, particularly if there was a belief that the school should have done more to support their child.

Where a learner has been supported by the school, the Connexions staff based at the school should complete a learner disabilities and difficulties (LDD) information form. This is completed in conjunction with parents and learners, but only when the student is known to the school's SENCO, because s/he has been receiving support at the stages of School Action or School Action Plus. The LDD form is then sent to colleges and training providers who received applications from the learner. The information passed on will include details of any statement of special educational needs or individual learning plan. This information is important as it gives staff an indication of the difficulties experienced by incoming students and the type of support that has been in place previously. It also allows staff the opportunity to plan the level of support for their next course of study. It enables mainstream tutors to be aware of differentiation that will need to be planned for lessons. Importantly, the information will identify whether a diagnosis of dyslexia or other difficulties has already been made. It is essential that learners, and the significant adults who are supporting them, share information with the prospective course teaching teams. This allows necessary support to be made available for the start of a course of study, but will be treated confidentially.

Initial assessment

When all of the students have enrolled, there will be a process of initial assessment (IA), which seeks to benefit students by identifying the right key skill level for each individual and by focusing teaching on their real needs. Many colleges now use a computer package that will give a baseline assessment of skill in literacy and numeracy and an indication of a level at which a learner is working. There are also paper-based assessment materials available. In addition to this, learners may be asked to complete a piece of free writing, producing as much as they can on a given topic. This can be administered by mainstream tutors but the resulting piece of work should be assessed by the learning support tutors. They will mark this in a consistent way, and it is good practice for this team to carry out moderation of the marking to ensure consistency. The exercise provides the opportunity to evaluate students' skills in planning a piece of writing, their use of grammar, syntax and punctuation, and most importantly, errors in letter structure such as letter reversals or spelling errors that may be phonetic in nature. These may indicate that a further diagnostic assessment would be recommended.

A simple self-assessment questionnaire is useful for identifying learners' perceptions of their own abilities and confidence in carrying out tasks, and this can be carried out at the induction stage by mainstream tutors, and referred to in learner tutorials as the academic year progresses. This information should be used by teachers to feed back to students both their strengths and their areas for development. There needs to be a constant dialogue between support tutors and the teaching team regarding learners' progress, and the useful strategies developed to support them. This will inform their Individual Learning Plans (ILPs).

Assessment implications

Who decides if a diagnostic assessment is essential? There will be students who will say that they do not need an assessment when either evidence from an initial assessment or submitted class work would indicate the contrary. We cannot force this upon them – they are in adult education and should be treated as adults. Any tutor can make a referral, possibly following a tutorial review of progress, and students can self-refer to discuss their difficulties by visiting the learning support area and asking to see a specialist tutor. Parents can also contact the student support service with concerns.

The purpose of the assessment is to determine whether access arrangements need to be put in place. An assessment also governs recommendations to teaching staff, who should encourage learners to feel comfortable with any such rec-ommendations. Guidance from assessment will also enable staff to support students using adaptations in the classroom.

Attainment scores in tasks carried out for the diagnostic assessment will be given as standard scores, or sometimes scores are shown as a centile level. This refers to the level of percentage, so that for someone who scores at a centile of 40, it means that 60 per cent of the comparable group would have done better on that particular task. Depending on the level of standard scores achieved in literacy assessments, extra time can be added for examinations and practical tasks.

If a learner attains a low score in single word reading and reading com-prehension as well as a low reading speed, then a reader can be provided. It needs to be made clear that in an examination a reader can only read the text in the exam and cannot offer any explanation of unfamiliar words. If a student's handwriting is illegible because of spelling errors or they have poor handwriting skills, or slow writing speed, then help from an amanu-ensis (a scribe) can be deployed to write down dictated responses. If a learner has sufficient word-processing skills, then the use of a word proces-sor can be provided. If any of this provision is in place, learners need the opportunity to practise with their reader and scribe, using unrelated work, prior to the examination. This not only helps the working relationship but also allows learners the opportunity to prepare themselves mentally and emotionally for the examination.

An assessment for learners on a National Diploma or access to higher edu-cation course may well mean that they will be applying for a Disabled Students' Allowance (DSA) to attend university. Learners who are studying on a Higher National Diploma (HND) in FE will require a DSA for support as this would not be covered under the normal funding arrangements for students in a college.

To access the Disabled Students' Allowance, an assessment has to be carried out by a specialist teacher with appropriate qualifications or an educational psychologist. The practitioner must hold an Assessment Practising Certificate issued by either the Professional Association of Teachers of Students with Specific Learning Difficulties (PATOSS), Dyslexia Action or the British Psychological Society. Practitioners will have their reports checked for a quality standard and must demonstrate a commitment to continuous professional development in order for their licence to be renewed every three years.

In further education, students studying on a Level 3 or 4 course, including an advanced modern apprenticeship, would need to be assessed as experi-encing a specific learning difficulty to be funded for support. Students study-ing on higher national diploma courses, or 2+2 degree courses (a course which supports access by having two years taught in a partner college, fol-lowed by two years in the university) or a postgraduate course, such as the Diploma in Training in the Lifelong Learning Sector (DTLLS) teacher training course, would need to apply to their local authority for a DSA.

The role of the support tutor

The skills of working on an individual basis with a learner involve establishing a sound relationship, which may take the first few sessions of tuition. It helps if students are encouraged to share ownership of the sessions by sharing the aims and objectives. The specialist tutor may ask students what they wish to gain from their support or enquire whether there are particular issues for which they want help. There should be time allowed in support lessons for learners to have an opportunity for personal reflection, but no more than about five or ten minutes. In addition to any particular study focus, lessons need to develop underpinning skills, such as phonemic awareness, assignment planning and proofreading techniques.

Many young people are seeking skills for a vocational qualification that will allow them to pursue employability and a career. Nevertheless, they may feel reluctant to challenge their own literacy skills and expose their weakness in the workplace, and may wish to stop short of working at their target level. Support tutors need to ensure flexibility in the planning of their lessons, making them relevant for learners by using coursework or referring to topics that are of interest, and working towards creating independent learning. Professionals in FE also need to remain aware that, although students may received a diagnosis of dyslexia, their individual difficulties affect them in different ways, and they may also experience co-occurring difficulties that have an impact upon learning.

Support tutors are not always vocational specialists. To ensure an all-round support for learners it is important to have good communication between specialist tutors, progress or personal tutors and subject tutors. They can give guidance on the scheme of work being followed and where complex work will be required of learners. Where recommendations have been made for specific reading or spelling programmes, progress and subject tutors can provide vocationally relevant material in order to contextualise the learning. This enables support tutors to help learners; for example, by compiling a glossary of vocational words and terms.

Progress/personal and subject tutors will also be able to give guidance on the structure of any examinations and likely topics. This is covered in general class revision sessions but needs to be shared with support staff. It is essential that students are prepared for their examinations. A negotiated revision plan for the support sessions, as well as a negotiated plan for the homework that is expected of learners, can be constructed, implemented and reviewed.

The debate: is there a difference between adult dyslexia and childhood dyslexia?

More students whose dyslexia was not understood or identified at an earlier stage in their education are now entering FE and HE. Adult learners will have developed compensatory mechanisms in literacy tasks, and there is an argument for considering adult dyslexia, with its established learning patterns, as different in its characteristics from childhood dyslexia, with its inherent developmental qualities. Research interest lies in the cognitive and neural characteristics that may be present in dyslexic adults, but there are also differences in professional practice. Adult dyslexia provision may consist of support in subjects and assistance with study skills and meeting targets, but is less likely to be directly concerned with implementing programmes such as those developing phonics skills (although sometimes lexical difficulties will require interventions of this kind). Finally, when adult learners are assessed, it is not appropriate to refer to reading or spelling ages; comparing these with chronological age is irrelevant.

Key technique: alternative assessments

It is helpful to consider the assessment process of a particular qualification and the ways in which a learner can present evidence of their knowledge. A written assignment may not present an accurate reflection of the learner's knowledge and perhaps an oral validation would support this. Apprentices on a work-based learning programme could be offered the opportunity to use video to present work-based evidence. When marking scripts it is important that practitioners ensure students can demonstrate an understanding of the subject, therefore the content is paramount.

The DDA Code of Practice (DRC, 2007) makes detailed provision for alternative assessments. This would enable practitioners to take the interesting opportunity of letting learners choose their own means of being assessed, as follows:

- For all methods, the same content, knowledge and skills would be assessed, the same learning outcomes applied, tasks would be of comparable length or effort, and the same marking criteria would be used.
- For all methods, there would be an underpinning short preliminary task such as a literature review, a chronology, the creation of an artefact or some other contextual task, depending on the field of study. This would be submitted at the same time as rest of the assessment.
- Students could then have the choice of, for example:

  i) an examination with a 'seen' paper
  ii) a set of short questions
  iii) a portfolio
  iv) a presentation
  v) a poster.

An innovative practitioner who was willing to give students a choice of even two or three of these may find, through providing this equality of opportunity, that there are benefits in terms of student application, commitment, confidence and outcomes.

What does the Code of Practice say about students in FE?

The *Disability Discrimination Act 1995: Code of Practice Post-16* discusses the duty not only to make, but also to anticipate reasonable adjustments for all post-16 students with learning difficulties and disabilities, describing this as 'a cornerstone of the Act' (DRC, 2007: para. 5.2). The only time this does not apply is in the case of competence standards. Where dyslexia is concered, it would be necessary to enquire whether literacy forms a real, or merely an assumed, competency standard in any specific field of FE or HE in which students are working.

 Case study: David; fearing for his job

David, aged 47, was employed as a warehouse operative. His work involved having to identify stock to be collected from the warehouse from a 'pick sheet' and taken to the loading bay. He also had responsibility to ensure the security of areas after this task was completed. David's employers had contracted with a Train to Gain provider to deliver National Vocational Qualifications (NVQ) Level 2 to their staff. David had been encouraged by his line manager and personnel officer to sign up for this. David's NVQ assessor soon realised that he might be dyslexic (David commented that he always had trouble with reading and writing, and attended special classes at school). The specialist teacher was asked to see David and a full diagnostic assessment was carried out. David expected this to lead to him losing his job as had happened in the past. He commented that he would never be able to read what was required of him in the NVQ standards, and certainly couldn't write about tasks that he had to carry out. He told of an occasion when he had difficulty filling in an application form and was asked to leave as he would be no use in the workplace.

The FE specialist comments

David should be reassured that he would not lose his job. David does not want his work colleagues to know of his dyslexia, so any assessment information should be shared only with his line manager and personnel officer. He should be supported in the workplace for one hour a week by the specialist teacher through additional support funding available for the Train to Gain programme. Although at first David may seem reluctant to follow a specific programme to deal with his underlying difficulties, he may be able to engage with learning through working with his support tutor, and through adjustments made in the workplace such as having 'TextHelp' on a workplace computer. Flashcards could be used in the support session to enable David to identify key words and sequences in the workplace.

The HE specialist comments

David needs his confidence re-building and perhaps an emphasis on dyslexia being a learning difference may help him to see his difficulties in a different light. A support tutor can search for areas of functioning, not just with work in which David is successful, and relate these to his dyslexia. If David has to read lists, an eye-level ruler of an appropriate colour (even if he does not suffer from visual stress) may help him to follow the correct data.

 ### Points for discussion

- The government has set an ambitious target for raising the skills level of the population. Does this put pressure on the teaching skills of non-specialist teachers?
- David needs confidence, knowledge of his disability rights and development of his literacy skills. Which should take priority?
- What could his mainstream tutors do to help David?
- What are the implications of David disclosing his disability in the workplace?

In due course, David's increased confidence in his computer skills meant that he could work semi-independently. Once David had increased his levels of confidence and self-esteem, he could engage in working on improving his reading and writing skills and could look forward to his educational achievement. Importantly, David is aware that he now has the ability to study beyond Level 2.

 ### Summary

1. Further Education is changing to meet the widest work and learning needs of the community.
2. Early recognition of difficulties will allow learners to receive appropriate support and advice as well as the opportunity to achieve their learning goals.
3. Supporting dyslexic learners is not just the responsibility of the specialist teaching team, but is the responsibility of all staff.

Further reading

Learning and Skills Council and the Department for Education and Skills (2007) *Delivering World Class Skills in a Demand-led System.* Coventry: LSC.

Leitch, Lord S. (2006) *The Leitch Review of Skill: Prosperity for All in the Global Economy – World Class Skills. Final Report.* London: HMSO.

Reid, G. and Kirk, J. (2001) *Dyslexia in Adults: Education and Employment.* Chichester: John Wiley & Sons.

Assistive software

The graphical representation at the start of this chapter is provided through the use of Microsoft Visio. This product can be purchased on licence and is a useful tool not just for creating graphic representations but also for scale drawings relevant to engineering and construction courses.

Student comment

'I've actually got a job now but I told them I'm dyslexic at the start though not quite sure whether I'm supposed to or not. It didn't come up in interview, then I think, probably all students are a bit worried about careers. This job is a structural engineering job. It's a really good company'. Charlotte

3

Dyslexia-friendly higher education

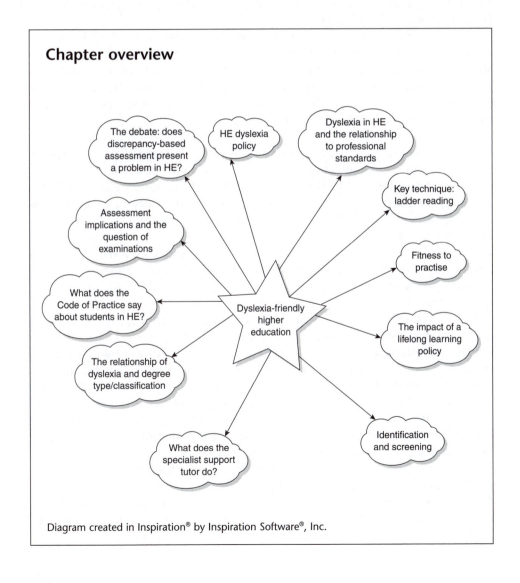

Chapter overview

The debate: does discrepancy-based assessment present a problem in HE?

HE dyslexia policy

Dyslexia in HE and the relationship to professional standards

Key technique: ladder reading

Assessment implications and the question of examinations

Fitness to practise

What does the Code of Practice say about students in HE?

Dyslexia-friendly higher education

The impact of a lifelong learning policy

The relationship of dyslexia and degree type/classification

What does the specialist support tutor do?

Identification and screening

Diagram created in Inspiration® by Inspiration Software®, Inc.

Dyslexia in HE and the relationship to professional standards

The purpose of higher education is changing; knowledge transfer, which in HE refers to the movement of academic knowledge and research out to other users such as industry, government, or the community, is now a significant part of the role of higher education. In tandem with this is the changing perception of students, who expect their degrees to enhance their eligibility of employment.

In addition to Widening Participation, Access and Aimhigher initiatives, HE institutions extend partnership to employers, both to support student numbers and to ensure that graduate students develop the skills that future employers need. Transferable skills are becoming an essential aspect of degree courses, and just as the ethos of HE is changing, so is the pedagogy. It can be argued that pedagogic accessibility through dyslexia-friendly approaches can lead to better outcomes for all learners.

It seems apparent to some academic staff that students at university expect to be emphatically 'taught', rather than just attend lectures. Focusing on the student view, Price and Skinner (2007) point out that students often expect more to be available from their personal and subject tutors. They expect support and reassurance in the drafting of ideas and the reading of extracts, and individual, academic tutorial support.

Many programmes at Bachelor's and Master's degree level will now routinely include some elements of study skills work. This ensures that students from a wide range of educational and work experience have the same understanding of scholarly skills. However, in addition to making study knowledge generally available, there are also issues raised by the duty to make reasonable adjustments in facilitating the literacy-based learning of dyslexic students. Some staff consider that reasonable adjustments may lower academic standards, but this may be due to a lack of understanding both of dyslexia and of how students experience HE. If consulted, disabled students could be the catalyst for improvement for all students, as reasonable adjustments that remove barriers to learning for a few can result in enhanced learning for all.

The Association of Dyslexia Specialists in Higher Education (ADSHE) suggests that distributing handouts prior to, or at the start of, the lecture is a reasonable adjustment for students with a specific learning difficulty (SpLD) because if a student has slow or illegible writing, it is impossible for them to keep pace with the lecturer. Handouts can help all students, as they allow concentration to be focused on the information the lecturer is imparting rather than on writing at speed so as not to miss important facts. However, Fuller et al. (2004) found that 44 per cent of their student sample did not receive handouts. Some lecturers have been known to remark that they fear that students will not attend their lectures if they have handouts either given in advance or made available to them electronically to view in their own time. Others may feel that they want the student concentrating on the presenter, rather than on reading handouts. Both of these views may be a matter of belief rather than evidence and neither perspective helps students with dyslexia.

As in FE, tutors and lecturers can be judgemental about spelling, grammar and syntax. Mitchell (2004, para) reports the words of one member of staff as 'I myself tend to be "bolshie" about grammatical errors despite their dyslexia', which suggests that students are sometimes punitively marked. Staff training on disability should inform academic staff about how to approach the marking of written work submitted by students with dyslexia. However, staff development is not always well attended.

Universities are enjoined to provide teaching courses for new members of academic staff which will help them to meet the learning needs of the changing student body. However, disability awareness training tends to be provided on a voluntary basis. The nationally-recognised course Teaching in Higher Education, which is assessed and fully accredited by the Higher Education Academy, is one such course but this deals with general pedagogical issues as a preparation for new teaching staff. Individuals wishing for further staff training about dyslexia can access the DEMOS project site, 'An introduction to students with dyslexia in higher education', (available online at http://jarmin.com/demos/course/dyslexia).

Students with learning difficulties and/or disabilities benefit from the setting up of systematic student support, since otherwise they are disadvantaged by having to 'conform to an alienating and ultimately self-destructive educational experience', (Smith, 2007). Students who cannot learn in such an environment will not achieve their potential and may withdraw or fail, and this would have consequences for their self-esteem, with a loss to the workforce and the knowledge base. As Chasty and Friel (1991: 12) famously suggest, if the child, or in this case, the student, 'doesn't learn the way we teach, can we teach him the way he learns, and then extend and develop his competence in learning?' This means adapting our pedagogy. Dyslexia-friendly practice should seek to put adaptations in place in the regular learning setting, in addition to following any recommendations from specialist tutors.

Fitness to practise

The issue of dyslexia among doctors and nurses is sometimes raised in considering the question of fitness to practise, coupled as it is with a fear of errors in treatment. The General Medical Council recommends reasonable adjustments, such as extra time in examinations, but with regard to clinical examinations, less scope is available because of the 'fitness to practise' requirement. This forms an element of assessment alongside assessments in theoretical and practical aspects of the subject, so that medical students may be considered confidently to be safe practitioners. Competence standards, according to the DDA, have to be applied equally to disabled and non-disabled students and although reasonable adjustments do not have to be applied to competence standards, they have to be made to the way competence standards are assessed.

A health care professional has to be effective, competent, safe and an independent worker. In contrast to assumptions, there is some likelihood that students who experience dyslexia may take extra care when checking medicines and interventions, just because of their knowledge of their own dyslexia. Before judgements are made about the fitness to practise of health care professionals, consideration should be given to comparison with error rates and inadequacies among non-dyslexic health care students. Health care managers could also consider how far conventions and practices could be altered to make the working environment more accessible; however this remains a target for the future. The General Medical Council (2008) provides advice about reasonable adjustments in the medical education sector.

The impact of a lifelong learning policy

'Lifelong learning can change people's lives, even transform them and that needs to be encapsulated in a learning culture for all' (Fryer, 1997, cited in Mitchell, 2004). This policy has implications for universities because, as people return to education, the number of students with dyslexia is expected to increase. The Higher Education Statistics Agency's (HESA) statistics show that over a period of 12 years the percentage of students with dyslexia increased from 0.4 per cent in 1994/95 to 2.8 per cent in 2006/07. There is no reason to believe that the number of students experiencing dyslexia will decrease over the next few years.

Meehan's (2008a) research found that in recent years, while more students were either thought to have, or are formally assessed as having, dyslexia at primary school, the number of university students assessed for dyslexia did not decrease. This confirms that the number of students identified as experiencing dyslexia in HE is indeed increasing, with both widening provision and earlier identification playing a part. This being the case, it seems certain that more students with dyslexia will be applying for the DSA, although there is continuing debate as to whether mild dyslexia should be identified and specifically funded under the DSA.

Identification and screening

Screening is a valuable process for identification, but is not carried out for all students as a matter of course, as it is in FE. Students in higher education at all levels of study on undergraduate and postgraduate courses can refer themselves or be referred by staff for a dyslexia assessment. Screening, usually undertaken by a dyslexia tutor, is used to assess whether a student should be put forward for a full dyslexia assessment by an educational psychologist or other suitably qualified professional. This has cost implications for a student or a funding body. The screening process can take the form of an extended interview, when a history of the student's education and difficulties in acquiring literacy, their study skills and any problems in other relevant areas are discussed and recorded. Some of the questions on the British Dyslexia Association's adult checklist (BDA, 2006) can be helpful and a useful template is available in Jamieson and Morgan (2008). Some tutors use a screener, such as the Dyslexia Adult Screening Test (DAST)

(Fawcett and Nicolson, 1998), or a computer-based screener, such as QuickScan/ StudyScan (Sanderson, 2000; Pico Educational Systems Ltd, 2008) or Lucid Adult Dyslexia Screener (LADS)(Singleton, 2001; Singleton et al., 2002).

Fraser and Zybutz (2004) reported the results of completed questionnaires of 28 ADSHE members and found that 75 per cent of the students screened by their departments went on to a formal assessment and that 90–95 per cent of them were found to have dyslexia. They also found that there was no association between the comprehensiveness of screening and successful identification. Screening proved to be not only an identification process but also an opportunity for students to meet support staff and discuss issues, in particular the emotional responses to the difficulties encountered in their studies.

The Specific Learning Difficulties Working Group (DfES, 2005) set out the Department of Education and Skills' guidelines for assessment of students in FE/HE and suggested a range of possible standardised tests to assess the cognitive profile and literacy/numeracy skills of students. During the assessment process an educational psychologist usually administers an IQ test such as the Wechsler Adult Intelligence Scale (WAIS) III (Wechsler, 1999) as well as literacy tests. IQ is considered a stable composite score of a person's overall intellectual ability, but its use in this context is controversial. This is both because IQ is not a measure of potential and does not predict performance, and because its value in HE assessment is based upon discrepancy theory. This interprets scores in terms of statistics describing under-achievement or deficits, but it is an approach which is passing out of favour in other areas of dyslexia assessment.

Once an assessment of a SpLD has been made, a student may apply for DSA. Students approach their LA (or in England, from 2009, Student Finance England or other funding body) and present evidence of their disability. A Needs Assessment is then funded whereby a student's study needs are assessed and a support package may be recommended. This can include specialist software, study skills tuition or other resources.

What does the specialist support tutor do?

At the HE level specialist support tutors do not often teach reading and spelling systematically; a student entering HE will already have a level of literacy that will have enabled them to negotiate the examination system, although experiential learning can also be considered. While a specialist support tutor may find anomalies that can be corrected, work is more likely to be in response to the arduousness of study or in response to other characteristics of dyslexia such as sequencing, organisation, and memory. Apart from carrying out screening and assessment, the specialist support tutor works to facilitate the learning of students with dyslexia. This involves developing the student's study skills strategies and, in particular, written skills within the context of a listening and stable environment, which enables the student to become more confident and independent in an academic setting. Specialist support tutors may also be involved in staff training, liaising with other staff across the university and occasionally talking with parents. In addition, the administrative aspects of student support, such as reclaiming costs from the LA's DSA funding, charting a student's progress in skill development and supporting students in applying for extensions or making appeals, may be part of a specialist tutor's remit.

Specialist support tutors meet students on a one-to-one basis and in the initial interview will work out an individual learning plan (ILP) which is then signed. A specialist support tutor will normally spend the majority of time on improving writing skills and ensuring that students are familiar with using any IT equipment or software awarded. Work may include multisensory teaching of other study skills, such as effective reading, organisation, time management, note-taking, revision and examination techniques.

Some students, particularly if they have recently received an assessment of dyslexia, may appreciate small group workshops where they can meet other students with dyslexia and discuss the strategies necessary to maximise their strengths. Students with dyslexia may also need to be supported on placement if their course requires it. For example, it might be necessary to support, for several weeks, a social work student working in a placement, or a nursing student working on a ward.

The relationship of dyslexia and degree type/classification

In 1999, Singleton stated that 1–2 per cent of students in higher education had dyslexia and that 40 per cent of these students would obtain good degrees – Upper Second Class with Honours or First Class Honours. However, this finding may change with the increasing proportion of students with dyslexia entering HE. Further research considers the relationship of degree classification to IQ level for students with dyslexia in HE (Meehan, 2008b). A study of 320 undergraduate and postgraduate students with dyslexia in HE from 2002/03 – 2005/06, of which 278 were undergraduates, indicated that full scale IQ is not related to degree level. In addition, students with dyslexia at any level of IQ did not, as a group, perform as well as non-dyslexic students, although this did not prevent individual students with dyslexia obtaining a good degree. Overall, given the difficulties that students with dyslexia experience, it may be that they are less likely to achieve their potential. This corroborates the study of Riddell, Wilson and Tinklin (2002) who found that disabled students were awarded poorer degree classifications.

Assessment implications and the question of examinations

Courses in HE may be assessed by coursework or examination or a combination of both. Examinations are based on the premise that a student's knowledge can be judged on written evidence in a stipulated time, while coursework may include essays, portfolios, in-class tests, practical laboratory sessions and write-ups or mathematical problem sheets. In HE, assessment is the basis on which an award is given or competence in practice is recognised. In addition, students receive feedback and staff can monitor the effectiveness of their own teaching methods. It is important that staff consider how the assessment of modules both supports learning and measures the learning outcomes.

As part of a reasonable adjustment for students with a SpLD, 25 per cent extra time in examinations is usually recommended by an educational psychologist or other suitably qualified professional. Why this extra time is given depends on the needs of the individual student: a slow reading rate or a need to re-read for comprehension may result in extra time being recommended to decode or understand the examination questions. Often staff assume that extra time is given for students to check their spelling, grammar and punctuation and if a student has mild dyslexia this may be possible. However, it should be under-stood that if students have severe dyslexia and, for example, are unable to select the correct spelling of a word from a drop-down list in a spellchecker, no amount of extra time will enable them to correct their spelling. Not being able to spell is a facet of their dyslexia which is a disability rather than a literacy problem and is much in evidence in a written examination.

Various options can be recommended by a needs assessor should a student need all or any of them, such as the use of a computer because of a slow writing speed or illegible handwriting, a reader if a student has below average reading rate (below 85 standard score, i.e. below the 16th percentile) or comprehension, coloured paper or a coloured overlay if a student experiences Meares-Irlen Syndrome or visual stress, a scribe if a student has difficulty holding a pen, or separate invigilation if they are receiving extra time.

Obviously, a module that relies solely on 100 per cent examination could put students with dyslexia at a disadvantage, hence there is a need for the method of assessment to be clearly stated in the module handbook and for alternative methods of assessment to be considered. Some students with dyslexia find it difficult to express themselves in written format, particu-larly under examination conditions. They may find it difficult to express their ideas or order information, and assignments may take up to ten times longer for them than for their peers. Fuller et al. (2004: 312) found that 33 per cent of students found examinations and coursework to be a barrier to learning because lecturers did not understand the anxiety involved in writing or the length of time that students with dyslexia needed to spend on assignments.

Students with dyslexia may appeal to student services for help, but disability officers may have difficulty influencing teaching and learning in HE insti-tutions. Academics may find it difficult to accommodate and provide extra support for disabled students. In particular, they may not agree with, or may not be able to arrange, alternative assessments. An alternative assessment means providing another way to test the learning outcomes of a module. For example, if the course is 50 per cent continuous assessment and 50 per cent examination, it may be a reasonable adjustment for a student with dyslexia to have an oral examination rather than a written examination.

HE dyslexia policy

In FE and HE, as in work settings, employers and service providers are enjoined not to discriminate against disabled people. The *Special Educational Needs and Disability Act* (DfES, 2001) requires universities to have a disability statement in which the policy and provision of the institute for students are outlined. This would take into account the reasonable adjustments for students with disabilities such as dyslexia, so that they should not be discriminated against. Institutional flexibility is needed and, in particular, listening to, and consultation with, disabled students is important, enabling student voices to be heard. In addition, within each HE institution there is need for a dynamic whole-institution policy which reflects the changing student body. A model for a dyslexia policy for FE or HE institutions is given in Appendix 3.

The debate: does discrepancy-based assessment present a problem in HE?

The discrepancy model of assessment describes the mode of assessment where the identification of dyslexia is confirmed as the result of a statistically significant difference between literacy skills and general IQ, or another factor. The size of the gap shown by the testing is measured, and where it is extreme, and where there has been adequate educational opportunity, the identification of dyslexia is made. However, there are criticisms of the concept of IQ and the discrepancy model of assessment of dyslexia is contested. This presents the higher education sector with a problem, because the position of students with dyslexia in HE is predicated upon the judgement that, were it not for their dyslexia, they would be functioning at a much higher level appropriate to HE, as demonstrated by their assessment measurements.

Discrepancy theory has become controversial because testing IQ is in itself contentious and also because IQ is not strongly related to reading. A low score on verbal IQ may mask a specific problem with reading, so that it is not identified, thus there is doubt about the use of IQ tests forming part of an assessment. However, the DfES SpLD Working Group (2005) reports that such a diagnosis (including IQ and literacy tests) gives further support to an assessment and notes that difficulties identified are evidence of underlying cognitive deficit, exclusive of other factors. The fact that the structure of dyslexia identification, provision and support within HE and, by association, within the LA's funding of resources for student support, is based upon a discrepancy process that may be used only in this sector, is increasingly problematic.

Profiling is an alternative to discrepancy-based assessment and some psychologists will submit reports that are based on profile and consultation rather than on test scores. Everatt, Weeks and Brookes (2008) suggest that it is the pattern of strengths rather than weaknesses that identifies a specific learning difficulty, and although a discrepancy is implied in this, it need not be a matter of measurements and test scores. Reid et al. (2008) confirm the heterogeneity of profiles of dyslexic adults. While profiling may present a more complete understanding of a dyslexic learner's individual needs, including support implications, it may present difficulties for a needs assessor, since the DSA is unlikely to be allocated unless the assessment process and report format follow the recommendations in the report of the SpLD Working Group.

Key technique: ladder reading

To cope with the higher quantity and level of complexity of reading tasks in HE, dyslexic students who experiencing a slower reading rate can be helped to access and manage their reading by the use of some simple reading skills. These can include scanning a page to locate topics of interest or skimming fast over text to identify quickly what is being communicated. This can be done by using a ladder read:

1   Read the first paragraph or introduction of a chapter or article.
2   Read the last paragraph or discussion/conclusion.
3   Read the first sentence of each paragraph in between.

The theory of a ladder read is based roughly on the Pareto Principle (otherwise known as the 80/20 rule), suggesting that if you read 20 per cent of the text you will have extracted 80 per cent of the information. In most paragraphs much of the meaning is in the first line, the rest is explanation, so the ladder read has a good chance of gathering most of the meaning.

What does the Code of Practice say about students in HE?

The *Disability Discrimination Act 1995: Code of Practice Post-16* (DRC, 2007) responds to changes in the disability legislation, as embodied in the Disability Discrimination Act 1995 (Amendment) (Further and Higher Education) Regulations 2006. While the Code focuses upon post-16 learning, in paragraph 1.4 it points out that its provisions also apply to higher education. Confirming the scope of this requirement it goes on to state:

> An educator's duty to make reasonable adjustments is an anticipatory duty owed to disabled people and students at large. (DRC, 2007: 227)

Case study: Sanjay; his obvious ability was not reflected in exams

Sanjay, aged 20, was a verbally proficient second year student studying for a BA in humanities. His tutors noted that he was active in discussions and debates and was able to make unusual connections between concepts introduced into the course modules. Sanjay was able to cope with his reading requirements through judicious use of methods to read efficiently, such as by using scanning and ladder reading, and by recording a summary of what he had read by means of a graphical representation. However, Sanjay's written examinations never reflected his potential; he was hampered by his slow speed of reading and written expression. His personal tutor suggested that he might have dyslexia and referred him to the disability office and after an assessment Sanjay was found to experience dyslexia.

The FE dyslexia specialist comments

As part of the assessment recommendations, the specialist assessor could ask for Sanjay to be given the opportunity to orally demonstrate his knowledge and understanding. This is acceptable in National Vocational Qualifications. There may also be the possibility of a scribe offered in examinations if his handwriting ability and writing speed were also impaired. An oral examination would have to be authorised by the examination board concerned.

The HE dyslexia specialist comments

Sanjay seems to have a high level of verbal intelligence and obviously has original ideas and a good understanding of his course. Students with dyslexia often find they cannot transfer onto paper in a fluent and logical way what they can communicate in speech. An oral examination would be a good alternative assessment arrangement for Sanjay and a reasonable adjustment on the part of his academic department.

 ## Points for discussion

- How would the academic tutor know that Sanjay was not just being lazy?
- What might be a reasonable adjustment in Sanjay's case?
- What about non-dyslexic students with high levels of verbal intelligence – how could the course assessment be made more inclusive?
- How would the specialist tutor prepare Sanjay for a written or oral examination?

At first, Sanjay's subject tutors were unconvinced about the advisability or indeed legitimacy of an oral examination, but the institution published a reminder to all staff that viva voce examinations can be allocated to students who are borderline for a degree classification. As a reasonable adjustment for his dyslexia during his final year, Sanjay was allowed to sit an oral examination after his written papers, enabling him to demonstrate the breadth of his knowledge and to discuss some of the topics constituting degree modules.

▢ Summary

1   If a student has been identified as experiencing dyslexia and has a report to this effect, staff must treat the student as having a disability.
2   All staff in HE need to be aware of disability legislation and to be anticipatory and consider reasonable adjustments; for example, considering alternative assessment arrangements when designing and implementing courses.
3   Increased communication between departments and disabled students will help academic staff to be more aware of the difficulties disabled students face and come to a decision about what might be termed reasonable adjustments for assessment on a case by case basis.

Further reading 📖

DuPre, L., Gilroy, D. and Miles, T. (2008) *Dyslexia at College* (third edition). London: Routledge.

Hargreaves, S. (2007) *Study Skills for Dyslexic Students.* London: Sage.

Jamieson, C. and Morgan, E. (2008) *Managing Dyslexia at University: A Resource for Students, Academic and Support Staff.* London: Routledge.

Assistive software 🖱

The graphical representation at the start of this chapter is provided through the use of Inspirations software. It is found on the Inspiration website and there is a free trial of the software at www.inspiration.com/Freetrial

Student comment

'I think I've always had a bit of difficulty with English but it was not until my second year at uni when a lecturer said, "You should have an assessment because your work doesn't make any sense to me and maybe it's something you should look into"'. Evan

Dyslexia-friendly written work

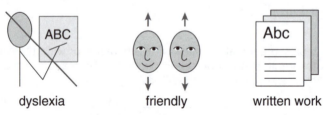
Scholarship and written exposition

Regardless of vocational or professional requirements, much of the knowledge conveyed in FE and HE programmes relies on written work to provide evidence of attainment. Although scientific and mathematical disciplines have requirements of their own, written work is still expected. Assessment, too, most frequently relies upon written exposition.

A considerable premium may be placed upon spelling as a signifier of good quality in written work. A whole range of academic opinion on this subject may be found, from the professional who is scornful of inaccurate spelling and sees it as a symbol of 'dumbing down', to the professional who believes that idiosyncratic spelling reflects the legitimate personal educational experience of the learner and should not be tampered with. Spelling is frequently the area in which difficulties of a dyslexic nature are manifest. Where learners experience mild or moderate dyslexia, reading skills may reach a useful level whereas spelling remains a more visible difficulty. The dyslexia literature, in seeking ways to help dyslexic learners, has explored spelling in detail and it is probably not surprising that much dyslexia scholarship has arisen in countries relying on the Roman alphabet and the deep orthography of the English language. This language has its origins in a number of language bases, all of which have made their mark on written and spoken English, leaving a system containing 26 letters which combine to make 44 sounds or phonemes. The arbitrariness of some of these combinations is demonstrated by the different soundings of the 'ough' combination, such as cough, through, thorough, and enough. All of these have alternative semantic expressions.

Zeigler and Goswami (2005: 19) confirm that within the Roman alphabet systems, 'English seems to lie at the extreme end of the consistency continuum with regard to orthography–phonology relationships', giving it a 'deep orthography', meaning that it is a complicated system, with complexity in both reading and spelling. It may be thought that this complexity would not have much impact upon a dyslexic learner who has reached the HE level of study. However, there is a possibility that students who experience dyslexia may make vocabulary choices that are safer, avoiding the use of what might be termed a 'mature' vocabulary, thereby losing the opportunity to demonstrate their scholarship to best advantage (Riddick, Farmer and Sterling, 1997: 169).

Punctuation, paragraphing and syntax, either in word choice or in word order, are all areas in written expression that can present difficulties for dyslexic students. These may be affected by wider-ranging characteristics associated with dyslexia, such as sequencing and memory. Lack of clarity in tasks, assignment titles or examination questions may divert or confuse dyslexic learners and affect written expression. Dyslexia-friendly practice expects that professionals will make tasks, titles and questions as clear as possible. Techniques like paragraphing and referencing can and should be taught as study skills; it is not fair treatment to expect these to be inherently understood or mastered by dyslexic students. Colleges and universities may have writing tutors or fellows to support students in their written work; nevertheless, providing direct teaching of such techniques within programmes meets the duty to anticipate the need for reasonable adjustments.

The nature of the written task

Between FE and HE the range of written tasks can be very great. In FE the smallest task might be the making of a few bullet points while the largest would be the writing of a traditional essay of 2000 words or more. In FE there will also be groups of students with more severe learning difficulties, whose literacy work is focused around a social sight vocabulary. Since dyslexia is not a function of IQ, it is likely that some members of this student group will also experience dyslexia and will particularly benefit from dyslexia-friendly approaches. In HE the smallest task might be the writing of a paragraph or two about an extract from a text, while the largest would be a PhD thesis of 80,000 words plus appendices. It seems as if one standard of quality is length or word count, although this may largely be a matter of convention or expectation within individual disciplines.

Of more concern for dyslexic learners is the expectation that they would be able to write spontaneously in the learning setting, whether by note-taking, answering a 'pop quiz' or undertaking some interactive task. Dyslexic students would have to confront this by marshalling both written expression skills, and, equally, confidence. For dyslexic students it would simply not be as automatic a process to write as it would be for non-dyslexic peers.

For some students in FE and HE, written tasks will be further complicated by difficulties with manipulation and coordination of writing implements. In the UK literature, handwriting difficulties are seen as a motor coordination difficulty subsumed within the general view of dyslexia, and may be described as dyspraxia or developmental co-ordination difficulty/disorder, co-occurring with dyslexia. In the US, a difficulty of this kind would be identified with the term 'dysgraphia', a term now becoming more visible in the UK. Statistically, around 50 per cent of people with dyslexia also experience dyspraxia (Deponio, 2004) and the unstable handwriting of someone with these difficulties may alarm professionals, so that the assessment of content may receive less attention. Fortunately, this problem can be eradicated by modern word-processing, and sensitive professionals can avoid springing unexpected writing tasks upon their students.

Note-taking is, however, another matter, as it is frequently seen as an academic skill. Study skills guides offer guidance, as does the *Framework for Understanding Dyslexia* (DfES, 2004). Individuals may develop their own method of note-taking; one student known to the authors takes notes electronically using Widgit software, as demonstrated at the start of this chapter.

Dyslexia-friendly practice would not expect copious note-taking and would provide scaffolding; in other words, a framework or structure, to support the process. A task to be avoided in dyslexia-friendly practice is that of setting students to copy quantities of notes from a board. Anecdotal evidence suggests that this can still happen, but it is surely a habitual, pre-technology technique that has no place in twenty-first century pedagogy, although the use of board work for exemplar material is acceptable. Many dyslexic students now prefer to use a small handheld recorder for the note-taking function, and it is becoming commonplace to see an array of these arranged near a lecturer or tutor. To refuse this convenience is of course to suggest that it is an unreasonable adjustment, which clearly is not the case.

Assessment of written work

Although the extended piece of writing in essay form is a common assessment requirement, other formats can be used if they relate to learning outcomes, can be marked, and make it clear to students how progress may be made. In the act of marking, one small change that can help dyslexic students is to avoid the use of red pen. This is because students with dyslexia have grown up having their scripts returned to them covered in red ink where literacy errors have been corrected by well-meaning practitioners. The result, however, creates aversion and demolishes confidence.

Marking itself can be problematic in the instance of students who experience dyslexia. As recommendations for adjustments, professionals who assess students for dyslexia and needs assessors may recommend how academics should consider marking student scripts. If spelling is being assessed then the percentage of the mark that may be deducted for poor spelling should be stipulated in the course prospectus so that students with dyslexia can make an informed decision about attending the course. Some colleges and universities issue stickers with which a student can endorse their work, so that the marker can take account of dyslexia. Other institutions do not use stickers, arguing that sufficient help is available for dyslexic students so that they will not need their scripts to be identified.

Sometimes a dyslexic student's assessment report will ask for sympathetic marking. However, this may challenge the institution's marking criteria, which generally include criteria concerned with presentation and written expression. This may present a problem for the marker, particularly where scripts are not anonymous. The marker may want to make allowances for dyslexic students, but feels that this may be unfair to others. One way to approach this is to consider spelling, grammar and syntax in terms of whether or not anomalies interfere with meaning. If they do not, this is less serious than if meaning is compromised.

All colleges and universities have their own marking criteria, but these are likely to be similar in order to ensure comparability across institutions. The criteria reflect the descriptors for the level that are embodied in the academic framework (QAA, 2001; QAA, 2008). These do not demand extended writing or flawless presentation per se; instead they refer back to the expectations within academic disciplines. The writing requirement is embedded within the subject discipline, an artefact of tradition and the historically accessible technology of the written word.

Markers should observe the marking criteria consistently for all students. However, experience suggests that matters of presentation and written expression should not, in general, be the reason for crossing the fine line between a first/distinction level mark and a lower band, or should not make the difference between a pass and a fail. In either of these cases the mark may be challenged by a student who feels that their dyslexia has not been sufficiently taken into account, and it would be difficult to justify the marker's position on matters of presentation alone.

The role of ICT and assistive technology

E-learning environments and enquiry-based learning can help dyslexic learners because they can access electronic sites in their own time, re-read as many times as they wish and respond at their own speed. While written work remains a part of this pedagogy, through the medium of the computer keyboard, the time is approaching when it may become necessary to question what we actually mean by written work. Speech recognition, spelling and grammar checkers, and cut-and-paste functions in word-processing programmes are changing what is meant by the term 'writing'. Further, the number, range and sophistication of assistive software programmes are continually increasing, and speech recognition and text-to-speech are now standard in word processor programmes.

The chapter openings within this book demonstrate some of the ways in which software can be used in planning or note-taking. Previously the province of the specialist tutor, these methods can be used by non-specialist teachers, tutors and lecturers, once they are aware of them. However, not everyone likes this type of graphical arrangement; some learners prefer lists. Although it may not be within the original intention, this kind of diagram can be converted to a list by numbering the terms, and this reveals something worth bearing in mind for teaching and learning with students who experience dyslexia – that is the prevalence, and consequently the assumption, of an expectation of linear, logical progression in knowledge, which is inherent in pedagogy. This can be simply demonstrated when asking a student where to begin in numbering a graphical representation; he or she may not start at the point assumed by the educator to be the logical beginning.

Few institutions now accept submission of written work in handwritten form; some insist that essays are word-processed. This raises the interesting question of word count, which has arguably changed with the widespread use of word-processing. One university gives the following advice:

> When words were counted manually, quotes would not be included as they were not the author's original words. You can still find lecturers, and guidance, specifying that quotes should not be included. Now that we count words through the word count function in a word-processing package, we usually include the quotations.
>
> The impact of this can be reduced by applying good practice in the use of quotations. A quote should only be used when the author cannot express the thought better him/herself, or when it is something where we want to see the original words – for example when it is a famous, or seminal, line. Generally, quotes should not be more than about five lines long without a very good reason. (Martin and Pavey 2008)

Students who have no other guidance can be advised to resolve any uncertainty by declaring whether their word count does or does not include quotations.

The role of libraries

As the nature of reading and writing tasks changes with technological advances, so too the role of libraries is changing and expanding. Library and information technology service staff can do a great deal to support learners who experience dyslexia and there are likely to be policies in place for this purpose. They may, for example, be willing to give extended loan periods for students who experience dyslexia or may be able to provide coloured overlays or tinted paper for copiers. A range of assistive software may be available in computer clusters and some libraries provide designated areas where speech recognition software can be used for dictation purposes. In order to provide these services, library staff will identify potential users through liaison with the student support team.

The College of Further and Higher Education group of the Chartered Institute of Library and Information Professionals (CILIP) provides a self-assessment toolkit for learning resources services in FE colleges (CILIP, 2008). This includes, within its quality standards, the expectation that there will be staff responsible for monitoring and promoting 'diversity and inclusivity' (para. 4.1) and that there will be facilities for learners with 'specific needs' (para. 4.2), that resources will be fully accessible, and that there will be disability training provided for learning resources staff. CILIP notes the possibly that libraries, being by their nature concerned with written text, may cause apprehension among dyslexic learners. Most interestingly, in looking to the future, CILIP notes the increasing range of ways that students access information, and calls for the recognition of the new demands that these make upon provision and resources, and the cross-boundary working that these require. Within FE and HE, library and information support services appear well-placed to meet the needs of dyslexic students, as long as they know who they are. It remains a question as to whether the range of adaptive methods and materials are available to all on request or whether they are linked to perceived deficit. Nevertheless the positive outlook sets a useful example.

The debate: is proofreading acceptable?

The issue of whether or not proofreading is permissible or whether it represents an unfair advantage is a topic which from time to time appears in the FE and HE trade press. Academics may feel that proofreading gives students an unfair advantage, because it helps them to overcome the difficulties that may be indentified in the marking criteria governing presentation. However, proofreading is likely to be one of the services carried out by the support tutor, because the type of mistakes that look like proofreading errors are characteristic of presentation that is affected by dyslexia. Proofreading is also one of the group of available study skills that is cited in the CILIP toolkit as a quality indicator of services provided by library and resource staff.

Concerns have also been raised about the provision of proofreading in other circumstances; companies offering proofreading as a purchasable service have been castigated. How much help is too much? This falls in the area where proofreading becomes correcting, and correcting becomes suggesting, and this relies on the tutor's professional judgement in avoiding telling students what to write. However, the provision of proofreading to students with dyslexia would fall within the remit of anticipatory and advantageous adjustments, and should therefore be accepted.

Key technique: structure the assignment

The style of academic writing that we require from students is not the only way to express content, and within academic writing there is a range of styles. Even at its most straightforward, conventional writing does not directly imitate thought or speech. Nevertheless, conventional essay writing allows the writer to demonstrate scholastic skills, including those of analysis and logical progression in the reviewing of materials and construction of arguments.

Sometimes learners, who may or may not experience dyslexia, arrive in FE or HE at a mature point in their lives. Students in this position may feel very anxious about carrying out an extended piece of writing and may have only their earlier experience to draw upon. While different disciplines have conventions of their own, for general purposes students value knowing that it is acceptable to write in the first person when the topic warrants it, and that it is usual now to include subheadings. Using subheadings in an essay aids the construction of the piece and the flow of argument can be improved by being able to move sections. Experience suggests that some basic techniques can also help, such as:

- Background → present position → way forward (for the content).
- Tell them what you're going to tell them, tell them, then tell them what you told them (for the structure, i.e. introduction, exposition and conclusion).

The template in Appendix 4 demonstrates how these techniques may be used to structure almost any essay using a Mind Map® (Buzan, 2007). This can be given a specific topic focus, and can be led by the tutor and carried out in the entire group or in an individual tutorial. Dyslexic and non-dyslexic students alike appreciate having their knowledge of how to construct an essay augmented, leaving them free to focus upon content and argument.

What does the Code of Practice say about written tasks?

Chapter Nine of the *Disability Discrimination Act 1995*: *Code of Practice Post-16* includes helpful guidance on teaching and learning, assignments and assessments. The Code makes the point that pedagogical practices should be designed to be accessible, and confirms that educators need to be accurate about when something is, or is not, a competence standard. For example, the Code confirms that 'a requirement that a student sitting a written exam must "write neatly" is not a competence standard' (DRC, 2007: para. 5.74).

 Case study: Ted; the missing sticker

Ted, aged 55, was a mature student with dyslexia, who had entered HE through the access route from FE. He had sought advice from his student support centre. The institution used stickers to endorse the scripts of students identified as experiencing dyslexia, and Ted had been issued with some of these. Ted managed his first year of higher education successfully, but in his second year he failed an assignment. On receiving his fail mark Ted wrote a letter of complaint to the programme director, claiming that he had been unfairly marked since the mark did not take account of his dyslexia. The programme director knew that markers normally fulfilled their duty to make reasonable adjustments. Assignments were marked anonymously in this institution and there was no sticker on the script; Ted's view was that it must have fallen off.

The FE dyslexia specialist comments

On this basis Ted should have his script re-marked, particularly if the content demonstrates good knowledge and understanding. Perhaps this features as a difference in FE where anonymous marking may not always take place. Ted's course teaching team would also be able to give support to his appeal on the basis of previous work completed and of course his support tutor would also be in a position to support an appeal.

The HE dyslexia specialist comments

It might have been better if Ted had first met with the disability coordinator in his department, school or faculty who is responsible for informing staff of the students

(Continued)

(Continued)

with disabilities studying their modules. If Ted commonly used a sticker for his coursework, then this should be taken into consideration and the coursework should be re-marked. If Ted is in regular communication with a disability case worker and/or a specialist tutor they may be able to write a supporting letter to the school/college.

〰️ Points for discussion

- Does it make a difference whether Ted forgot to use his sticker or whether it fell off accidentally?
- Ted could have resubmitted the assignment and achieved a pass mark. Why did it matter to him so much, that he wanted to challenge the first mark?
- Should the programme director have agreed to have the essay re-marked?
- Does the kind of a student that Ted was perceived to be make a difference – for example, if he was seen as being diligent as opposed to indifferent or disrespectful?

The outcome was that although regulations supported the marking process so that complaints made on the basis of marking were not accepted, on this occasion Ted was given the benefit of the doubt and his essay was re-marked. Subsequently, Ted was always careful about using his stickers and went on to gain his degree with a 2:1 classification.

⬜ Summary

1   There is a considerable range of written tasks in FE and HE, but both sectors rely on written work in the acquisition and demonstration of knowledge and understanding, and in assessment.
2   There is potential to be far more flexible in the design and use of written tasks. They are not mandated by the academic framework, except for their part in a subject's discipline.
3   There is scope for FE and HE provision to be dyslexia-friendly without compromising standards. Library and resource services provide valuable support.

Further reading

Connelly, V., Campbell, S., MacLean, M. and Barnes, J. (2006) 'Contribution of lower order skills to the written composition of college students with and without dyslexia', *Developmental Neuropsychology*, 29 (1): 175–96.

Price, G. (2006) 'Creative solutions to making the technology work: three case studies of dyslexic writers in higher education', *ALT-J, Research in Learning Technology*, 14 (1): 21–38.

Strunk, Jr, W. and White, E. (2000) *The Elements of Style* (fourth edition). London: Longman.

Assistive software

The graphical representation at the start of this chapter has been carried out using Widgit Software's 'Communicate in Print 2' version 2.65/a, which is designed to improve communication and literacy. Widgit Software produce a range of symbol programmes and tools for communication. Widgit Software's website can be acccessed at www.widgit.com/

Student comment

'If you wanted feedback; it wasn't really there and if you're writing something you wouldn't be able to show a draft – have a draft-you just submitted your final piece and there was no sort of second chance. Obviously in an exam that's the nature of the thing but with your coursework you should get a progression of help'. Mel

5

Dyslexia-friendly laboratory and bench work

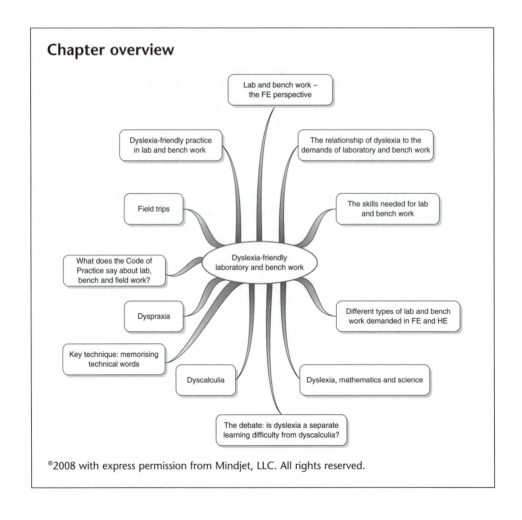

Chapter overview

Lab and bench work – the FE perspective

Dyslexia-friendly practice in lab and bench work

The relationship of dyslexia to the demands of laboratory and bench work

Field trips

The skills needed for lab and bench work

What does the Code of Practice say about lab, bench and field work?

Dyslexia-friendly laboratory and bench work

Dyspraxia

Different types of lab and bench work demanded in FE and HE

Key technique: memorising technical words

Dyscalculia

Dyslexia, mathematics and science

The debate: is dyslexia a separate learning difficulty from dyscalculia?

The relationship of dyslexia to the demands of laboratory and bench work

Some students with dyslexia can excel at practical work. Laboratory and bench work, workshop sessions and field trips all allow for multisensory learning by the application of principles already introduced in lectures and classes, making the learning experience more 'concrete'. However, dyslexia-friendly approaches require that the impact of dyslexia upon lab and bench work must be fully understood.

In the first instance, following a written procedure requires reading accurately and this can be a slow process of decoding and comprehending what is required. When there are time constraints and if a student is anxious, there is more possibility of misreading text and consequently making a mistake in an experiment which may not be rectified in the session. If students are working in pairs or groups this can put an added burden on students with dyslexia because if they misread an item such as an instrument dial or the chronometer timing a reaction, this will impact on their fellow students and anxiety will exacerbate the expression of dyslexia.

A lack of organisation can be a problem in practical work as most procedures have to be followed in a prescribed fashion. If many students are using the laboratory at the same time, it may be necessary to plan when specific equipment, for example, balances or spectrometers, are used. If a student has a poor working memory then it can be time consuming returning to the bench to re-read the manual for the next step in the procedure. A certain amount of mathematics may be an aspect of practical work and it may only be possible to calculate answers during the session, but for students with dyslexia, misreading or copying formulae or numbers incorrectly (such as mistaking 6 for 9 or 2 for 5) can lead to an invalidated experiment.

It should also be noted that students studying science subjects may have a heavy workload because they usually carry out one or two three-hour practical sessions per week in addition to attending their hours of lectures and tutorials. Towards the end of a term students with dyslexia can become very fatigued with the amount of concentrated brain work that is required and may need to sleep for a while after a day's work before being able to engage in more study.

In both FE and HE, in order for students to be successful in laboratory and bench work they must be able to follow a written protocol and keep in mind the steps of a procedure and follow it. Manual dexterity is required in procedures such as the making of solutions of chemical samples, and careful handling may be required in the use of delicate and expensive equipment such as specialist optical or electronic instruments. Numeracy and literacy skills are required to calculate concentrations and provide information to balance chemical equations. Accuracy in reading equipment scales may also be important and mathematical calculation may be a necessary part of an experiment. Consequently, in addition to literacy, some of the overlapping learning characteristics that can be associated with dyslexia, in this case dyscalculia and dyspraxia, can also have a bearing upon a dyslexic student's success in laboratory or bench work at any level.

The skills needed for lab and bench work

Experiments are designed for the average student to be able to finish within the time and note all relevant observations, draw graphs and gather any other results that may be needed to write up the experiment. Thus, students need to be able to organise their time and plan experiments in a timely fashion. A booklet (practical handbook) detailing the experimental procedures for the course may be made available to students at the beginning of the module so that it may be possible for them to read and plan their work efficiently before the lab session. Sometimes a talk is given before students start an experiment, outlining the risks and safety issues or noting any changes in the experimental procedure from that set out in the booklet, and emphasising the order in which the schedule has to be followed. Although it is important for students to complete the experimental procedure, it is more important for them to understand the principles underlying the experiment, to judge or estimate the value of the outcome of their work, and perhaps to rectify any mistakes made in carrying out the procedure, such as diluting a solution incorrectly.

Demonstrators are usually available during a practical session to oversee a class and give guidance to students but the onus is on the students, even if an experiment is conducted in pairs or groups, to organise themselves to achieve the goals for the session. It is clearly advantageous to have a good working memory, so that the procedure does not have to be continually checked.

Different types of lab and bench work demanded in FE and HE

Practical laboratory sessions have always been a component of science courses in HE and FE, and are a vital aspect of apprenticeships for trades. The nature of these sessions differs according to the discipline and the particular module studied. Examples might include the preparation of a particular chemical and its analysis, the generation of electricity or the taking apart of a car engine and its reassembly.

Laboratory sessions are designed to demonstrate theory and give students practical experience of what has been taught in lectures. They usually occur around the same time as the theoretical input. The skills developed in laboratory work are almost always essential for students who want to progress to a career in industry, trades or academic research. Obtaining a pass mark on the practical component as well on the theoretical assessment is usually a requisite of passing the module and obtaining course credits. Whether the labs are for biology, chemistry, medicine, nursing or engineering, there are certain common approaches that all students need to acquire in order to be successful.

In addition, the biological and geographical sciences often include field trips varying from an afternoon or day to a residential stay of a week or months in the UK or abroad for final year projects. Medical sciences, nursing and social science courses also have placements lasting weeks or even months, where students put into practice what they have been taught and are required to meet the competencies and skills needed for their profession.

Lab and bench work – the FE perspective

There is a number of workshop and bench activities carried out in FE courses. Construction programmes and craft areas are expected to use practical workshops. Students working towards a National Certificate Award will have to use specialist equipment, such as a theodolite (the instrument used in land surveying for measuring horizontal and vertical angles). Students on these courses may well progress to university to work towards a degree in architecture or surveying. Electricians have to demonstrate their knowledge of power ratings and flow of electricity. Vehicle engineering students have to demonstrate knowledge of the technical aspects of how the engine, brake and electrical systems work. Electronic and mechanical engineering both include complex practical work. There are other National Certificate courses such as forensic science that, in addition to the scientific aspects, will expect the learner to demonstrate knowledge of the law.

Although assessments in these areas are practical, there are now online multichoice exams to be completed for achieving some awards. Learners with dyslexia will have access arrangements for these, but the arrangements would also apply to practical assessments. There could be the opportunity to demonstrate subject knowledge orally in this situation and where a portfolio of work has to be completed, a scribe could be allocated to help students to complete this.

It is essential that non-specialist teachers, tutors and lecturers work with support staff to ensure that the tasks are sequenced and presented to the learner in a format that is easy to follow. The use of interactive websites such as Moodle or WebCT gives learners and support tutors the opportunity to access course material online, which is ideal for support, revision planning and preparation. They can also be used as communication tools between students and staff.

Dyslexia, mathematics and science

As there is less written work involved in science courses, students with dyslexia, but with ability in mathematics, may tend to select science degrees. Various attributes are necessary to make progress in mathematics, such as understanding numbers, counting, simple arithmetic, procedural methods, estimation, understanding mathematical language and problem-solving. Although students with dyslexia may have problems with arithmetic, this will not prevent them from understanding mathematical concepts and being successful in science.

Science involves stepwise learning, where skills acquired on the first step are needed to work through the second step and so on. Students with dyslexia may need to spend more time reviewing and reinforcing new material at one level before moving on to the next level. Students with dyslexia who are reading for degrees in biological sciences may have difficulty remembering and spelling unfamiliar Latin-based words, and chemists/biochemists may have difficulty with the nomenclature of organic or biochemical compounds. The volume of material and the speed at which it is delivered may be exhausting, and new students may have to give special attention to pacing their studies and managing stress.

Dyscalculia

In addition to any difficulties that mathematics may present to dyslexic students in the reading and writing of text associated with the field of study, there is also a body of opinion that considers that there is another specific learning difficulty termed dyscalculia, which focuses upon numerical and mathematical processes alone.

In 2003 Chinn stated that the research into dyscalculia was 20 years behind that of dyslexia. There are similarities in how dyscalculia has come to be understood and there are similar difficulties in its definition. Kosc (1974) defined developmental dyscalculia as a difficulty only in the area of mathematics when development of other cognitive functions is appropriate to age. It is considered to be genetic or congenital and neurological, and affects 3–6 per cent of the population (Shalev et al., 2000). Like dyslexia, estimates of this kind vary, however, and are related to how the term is understood and assessed.

As with dyslexia, the definition of dyscalculia emerged from the medical model and was first observed in patients suffering brain injury as a result of, for example, a stroke. Indeed there are certain syndromes, such as Turner's or Gerstmann's, which have mathematical difficulties as symptoms. However, compromised mathematical skills may also be attributed to the experiences of past teaching and learning, or to 'mathematics anxiety' making it difficult to ascertain whether a learner's problems with mathematics include a separate specific learning difficulty in this area.

Reading is not considered to be an innate skill, having been a relatively recent, culture-related aspect of human development; rather, it is a skill to be learned. However, there is evidence to suggest that we have an innate ability as infants to assess the number of items in a set (numerosity). This forms the basis of arithmetical skills and lack of this ability contributes to mathematical difficulties (Ansari and Karmiof-Smith, 2002).

Adults who experience dyscalculia have difficulty with simple arithmetic; for example, with operations such as single digit addition or subtraction, and they may rely on finger counting to find answers to arithmetical questions. Interpreting graphs is problematic, particularly if several different scales are used, and students may resort to wild guesses rather than being able to give a precise answer. Using money is difficult as it is hard to calculate the total sum of any purchases or to estimate the expected change.

The identification of dyscalculia is affected by the same complexities that govern the assessment of dyslexia. A screener for the 6–14 age range was devised by Butterworth (2003). An adult dyscalculia screener, DyscalculiUM, is at the trial stage but at the time of writing is not yet available. Both screeners have certain tests in common: numeracy, arithmetic and numerical stroop (a test where the size of a numerical figure does not reflect its value and the individual tested has to determine which is greater). In addition, DyscalculiUM contains tests on navigation, abstract thinking and the interpretation of graphs (Trott and Beacham, 2006).

Dyspraxia

The term 'dyspraxia', also known as developmental coordination disorder (DCD), often characterised by 'clumsiness', was identified by Orton in 1937 and describes a specific learning difficulty affecting fine motor control. DCD may also affect other areas of development including the acquisition of learning and is present in approximately six per cent of the population (Kirby et al., 2008). Adults with DCD may have difficulties with manual dexterity, handwriting, working memory, concentration and information processing, and these may co-occur with other specific learning difficulties. An adult diagnosis is often difficult because of a lack of standardised tests.

It is possible that students with significant DCD or dyscalculia may choose not to pursue, or may be guided away from, subjects that are highly science- or mathematics-based because of the demands that they make upon learners in areas where they experience specific difficulties. However, courses that are more theoretically oriented can enable students to show skills and knowledge to advantage. Further, if prospective students with dyspraxia, dyscalculia, and/or dyslexia meet the admission requirements for skills, qualifications and knowledge, they should not be discriminated against if they choose any science or mathematical programmes of study. Questions of capacity to follow the programme then become matters for consideration as to whether this would require reasonable or unreasonable adjustments.

Field trips

Fieldwork and residential courses can be an important part of science programmes, but they may present dyslexic students with particular challenges. Any difficulties that students with dyslexia express when in a learning environment will impact across all aspects of life and this may be very evident in a residential course. For example, there may be difficulties with punctuality, being able to meet at certain locations, the reading of schedules or the filling in of any necessary forms. In the interests of inclusion, module organisers should consider what are the learning outcomes from a field trip and explore alternative arrangements to make the experience equally accessible and valuable for students with disabilities.

Hall and Healey (2005) noted that some students with dyslexia found geography fieldwork difficult because of the organisational aspects of the timetable in a new environment where memory 'anchors' were not present. This added stress can exacerbate dyslexic tendencies, making dyslexic students less able to learn or to benefit fully from the practical aspects of the discipline. Note-taking in the field is reported as a particular problem because of the lack of time available. In these situations students may make only 'scrappy' notes which may not be sufficient to give a good write-up, and the field situation may not allow the use of an audio recorder.

In addition, reading materials necessary for the tasks to be fulfilled within a specified time may be difficult for students with dyslexia and take more time which may impinge on students' enjoyment of any leisure time built into the field trip or residential course. Time limits for any writing that has to be completed before the end of the event can also be a barrier to learning and pose particular difficulties for students. This is especially important if the field trip experience forms part of a dissertation project.

Dyslexia-friendly practice in lab and bench work

In supporting students with dyslexia, who may or may not also experience DCD or dyscalculia, when designing practical sessions we can put the following into action.

- Make sure that there is sufficient time for students to complete experimental work and try to allow more time for students who may take longer to finish, perhaps in another module's time allocation if there is space.
- When writing practical manuals, where possible, use a clear 12-point font and break up text using bullet points, subheadings, diagrams, flow charts and other graphically organised materials.
- If text or diagrams are imported or pasted into the practical handbook make sure these are of good quality.
- Make sure the steps in the experiment follow a logical sequence and are written in language that is not unnecessarily complex, using a larger font and bold lettering.
- Signal where steps may have to be modified due to differing conditions; for example, where a varying concentration of a solution may be available.
- Give out experimental manuals before laboratory sessions start so that students can read and plan the session beforehand, and can then make the best use of the time available to finish the experiment.
- Provide students with the opportunity to repeat processes that have been demonstrated, if necessary, in order to achieve fluency.
- Apply flexibility in giving dyslexic students extra time to help them to consolidate their learning.

- Allow extra time to write up experiments. Sometimes it is required that experiments be completed, written up and handed in during the practical session. It is important to make sure that this is absolutely necessary and if possible to allow the student with dyslexia to hand in the written work later (although once set, a deadline for all written work to be submitted has to be applied).
- Give the written procedure of a laboratory session on paper of a different colour. This enables it to be identified easily among other papers, since dyslexic learners will not find it so easy or speedy a process to pick out papers from text alone.
- Put contingencies in place for a student not obtaining the correct results or losing the physical object of an exercise or experiment; for example, if a chemical product made during a practical session is lost. This could perhaps be in the form of replacement data for them to analyse. The percentage of marks for losing data should be indicated in the course handbook.

The debate: is dyslexia a separate learning difficulty from dyscalculia?

If dyslexia involves transposition of letters, symbol confusion and poor working memory, there is no reason to suppose that this will not also occur with numbers as well as letters. However, Willburger et al. (2008) found that dyscalculic children had a specific difficulty with rapid naming of quantities, whereas dyslexic children had difficulty with rapid naming, and children with a co-occurrence of dyslexia and dyscalculia experienced an additive deficit. In addition, Butterworth and Yeo (2004) found that dyscalculic children were no different from a control group on forward and reverse digit span tests (these are tests that assess working memory by recalling strings of numbers), whereas dyslexic children found these tests difficult. It seems that students with dyslexia may often have problems with mathematics as well as language, and there may be an overlap between students with dyslexia and dyscalculia. There may certainly be a group of students with dyscalculia who have a problem only with mathematics. As Dowker (2004, abstract) states, 'if dyscalculia implies an impairment in all aspects of arithmetic and only in arithmetic, it would appear to be very rare'.

Key technique: memorising technical words

The principle of this technique is to attach the hard-to-remember word to something that is easier to remember because it is in a different mode (visual), is personal, is constructed for the purpose and may be humorous or bizarre, and therefore more memorable.

1 Segment the word to be memorised into chunks of two, three or four letters.
2 Allow the student to create a visualisation or association with each chunk.
3 Add the visualisations into one picture.

For example, the word 'Lepidoptera', the word for the order of butterflies and moths could be segmented thus: Le/pi/do/pt/era:

Le = French for the
pi = π
do = doing
pt = physical training
era = a particular age

The completed picture could be the butterfly with a π symbol on each wing doing physical training during the French Revolution!

What does the Code of Practice say about lab, bench and field work?

The *Disability Discrimination Act 1995: Code of Practice Post-16* shows how the making of anticipatory and reasonable adjustments should be applied in practical study contexts. In acknowledging the part that may be played by competence standards, it points out that reasonable adjustments may still be made. The code gives this example:

> A student whose disability affects his manual dexterity is allowed to use an assistant to measure chemicals and set up apparatus under his instruction for an assessment in chemistry. This is likely to be a reasonable adjustment. (DRC, 2007: 175, para. 9.35)

 Case study: Portia; can colour-coding be used?

Portia, aged 31, was a mature science student with dyslexia who had particular difficulties with symbol confusion and number reversal. Portia had no problems with grasping and understanding mathematical concepts and enjoyed working with numbers, but her difficulty in reading and writing symbols accurately prevented her from reflecting her understanding. After starting her course she found that she could not keep pace with copying some lectures off the board where 'chalk and talk' was still the mode of lecture delivery. After seeing a casework adviser, he contacted her needs assessor and asked for a note-taker for some of her lectures. Not having to concentrate on copying from the board relieved her of anxiety and she could focus on understanding the content of the course. Flashcards were her most effective way to revise, and in order to remember formulae Portia would give each of the symbols particular colours. Her difficulty was exacerbated in examinations, particularly if a calculation carried over onto the next page so Portia asked if, on her answer booklet, she might mark symbols and mathematical answers with colours so that she could follow her work more easily.

The FE dyslexia specialist comments

This case study demonstrates Portia's 'normal way of working' which has to be considered when making recommendations for access arrangements. Colour coding will help her to see if she has made any errors in directionality and sequencing when carrying out calculations. Guidance from subject tutors and her support tutor would ensure that she is able to use this correctly under examination conditions.

The HE dyslexia specialist comments

Allowing a student to use colours to avoid confusion with various formulae and intermediate answers to mathematical calculations is a reasonable adjustment. Portia should speak to her personal tutor, the subject tutor and the disability coordinator to agree examples of how her work should be set out in order that it could be read clearly by markers or external examiners.

∿ Points for discussion

- Is it important to distinguish between dyslexia and dyscalculia?
- Is there any reason for her teacher, tutor or lecturer not to agree to Portia's use of colour coding?
- Should Portia's tutor or marker be looking out for number reversals and giving her the benefit of the doubt?
- Could the tutor use oral questioning to determine Portia's understanding?

The outcome was that Portia found that she could keep track of her examination answers more easily using coloured pens and she also found it easier to estimate the expected answer. This decreased her examination anxiety and she found it much easier to check her answers before the end of the examination.

▢ Summary

1 Reasonable adjustments should be made for students with specific learning difficulties (SpLDs) in the area of practical laboratory sessions and bench work.
2 Difficulties with arithmetic or manual dexterity do not mean that students cannot achieve and even excel in practical courses.
3 Students with SpLDs studying courses which involve heavy workloads can become increasingly exhausted as the term progresses, which may impinge on the quality of their work.

Further reading

Butterworth, B. (1999) *The Mathematical Brain*. London: Macmillan.

Trott, C. and Wright, F. (2003) 'Maths and dyslexia in further and higher education', in D. Pollack, (ed.) *Supporting the dyslexic student in HE and FE: strategies for success.* Proceedings of a one-day conference held at De Montfort University and the University of Hull in June 2003.

Yeo, D. (2003) *Dyslexia, Dyspraxia and Mathematics*. London: Whurr.

Assistive software

The graphical representation at the start of this chapter is provided through the use of Mind Manager. It can be found by contacting Mindjet at: www.mindjet.com

---

Student comment

'I like maths a lot. Maths, it's interesting but it does take me a while to read things off the page. In maths you're writing down equations and I couldn't get the characters in – and drawing diagrams – in lectures I was always behind the rest of the class in terms of copying things off the board. I was always asking, "Oh! Could you leave it on the board a bit longer?", or I'd have to ask if I could borrow someone else's book. I was always getting stressed because I was slower than everyone else but once I had a note-taker for all my lectures, it was really helpful and I enjoyed the experience of learning'. Chris

The post-14 context

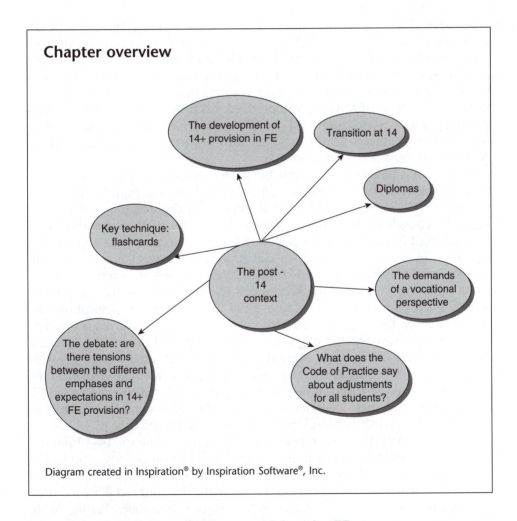

Chapter overview

The development of 14+ provision in FE

Transition at 14

Diplomas

Key technique: flashcards

The post - 14 context

The demands of a vocational perspective

The debate: are there tensions between the different emphases and expectations in 14+ FE provision?

What does the Code of Practice say about adjustments for all students?

Diagram created in Inspiration® by Inspiration Software®, Inc.

The development of 14+ provision in FE

There has been a growing partnership with schools, colleges and training providers for a number of years, which has seen Year 10 and Year 11 learners spend part of their education time in other education facilities. In recent years FE provision has been offered as an alternative to schooling for some pupils.

Dearing's *Review of Qualifications for 16–19 Year Olds* (1996) suggested that the FE curriculum being offered was too narrow. It needed to be broader to allow the country to develop the skills base of its young people and prepare for being able to compete in the modern global market. At the same time there was an awareness of disengagement from education for some young people, whom it was felt might benefit more from the opportunity to learn vocational skills, than from continuing to follow the school-based National Curriculum. It was felt that young learners experiencing difficulties, both academically and socially, could be given the motivation to learn and to develop skills that would increase their employment potential, if they were studying in the more vocational setting of the FE college.

Learners who were younger than the traditional FE entry age of 16, began to be placed in FE colleges in1999/2000 as part of a social inclusion initiative resourced by the UK government Standards Fund. The perception of college staff was that young people being sent on these courses were perhaps those less likely to succeed academically or those who challenged the school discipline system. This was confirmed, as schools used this new provision for their challenging pupils. Courses such as those in construction and light vehicle engineering were popular, with the practical nature of these courses making them attractive to less academic learners.

While pupils placed in FE might have been verbally prepared, often they were not aware of the difference in educational style to be found in their new placement. The differences in FE were evident in the teaching style, which might be considered less formal, and the lack of a bell that signalled break times. School finances were not structured to pass on money received for the education of young people with special educational needs, and there was no mechanism for transfer of funds from a school setting to a college setting, while retaining pupils on the school roll. Neither did LAs have a transfer system for support funding, because, from 1999, control of education had passed to a new funding administrative body, the Learning and Skills Council. Consequently, learners who might have been supported in school would not necessarily receive that same support in a college, although class sizes were smaller. There was concern over the safety of the new student group within the general college population. Some young people, manifesting behavioural difficulties, found that these were not managed in the same way as was the case in schools, and they swiftly found themselves rejected by the college.

Since 2004, with the final report of the Working Group on 14–19 reform, under Lord Tomlinson, the UK government has been following a project of reform for the later school and tertiary years aimed at developing the skills of the modern workforce. The Further Education and Training Act 2007 reflected the recomendations of the White Paper, *Further Education: Raising Skills, Improving Life Chances* (DCSF, 2006), changing the way that FE is funded and including closer links with employers. This project has changed the parameters of post-14 education. The purpose of the reform is a social and economic one, and in practical terms is intended to smooth the transition between compulsory and post-compulsory education, as a part of a lifelong learning perspective. Key Stage 4 (14–16-year-olds) is developing as a curriculum area in its own right. However, Brown and Pollard warn that:

> Such a change might not be helpful if the age of 14 were to become a new watershed and the continuity and coherence of prior education were to be disrupted at a new point of transition. (Brown and Pollard, 2006: 5)

This is something to watch out for in the coming years as the post-14 initiative unfolds.

McCrone, Wade and Golden (2007) produced a report based on research visits to five FE colleges, examining the strategies used to integrate Key Stage 4 learners and to consider the impact of 14–16-year-old learners on the institutions. The key findings were that 'significant successes' had been made in including these learners amongst the general college population. To enhance this, the report recommended the sharing of staff training days.

The overall response from older learners and lecturers was that the young people were now accepted into the college population and that they felt no significant impact from this group. Staff attitudes had changed, becoming attuned to younger learners as the courses progressed over the years. A greater awareness had developed of the skills required in teaching this group of learners and the challenges that could be faced in managing behaviour. The benefits to the younger group became clearer, such as the opportunities that the 14+ courses provided to inform choices in selecting an appropriate post-16 course. However, anecdotal evidence suggests that some young learners with dyslexia are still experiencing difficulties within the college environment.

Diplomas

The opportunities for 14+ education in FE were reformed partly as a result of the government's policy of loosening the restrictions placed by the National Curriculum on Key Stage 4, so that more educational choices could be offered at that stage, and partly because of other concerns about national levels in basic subjects and key skills. These changes reflected long-standing debates about the nature, relevance and attractiveness of vocational education. The Department for Education and Skills set out the rationale and timetable for the delivery of the new curriculum at Key Stage 4 and introduced new diplomas. There will be a total of 17 diplomas available for young people to choose from. They are being introduced gradually:

September 2008:

- Information technology
- Society, health and development

- Engineering
- Creative and Media
- Construction and the built environment

September 2009:

- Environmental and land-based studies
- Manufacturing and product design
- Hair and beauty studies
- Business administration and finance
- Hospitality

September 2010:

- Public services
- Sport and leisure
- Retail

September 2011:

- Travel and Tourism
- Science
- Languages
- Humanities

Aimed at raising the general skills level of the workforce in order to meet global competition, the diploma progression routes are intended to ensure that young people are engaged at levels that suit their ability. They encourage students to continue to develop skills; for example, by following an apprenticeship through to higher education.

The diplomas can be studied at three levels, up to Advanced level, and these will be recognised by higher education institutions as acceptable entry qualifications. Each level of the diploma will have equivalence to a number of GCSEs and A levels. The subjects of the diplomas reflect the occupational sectors of the economy and are supported by employer-led Diploma Development Partnerships (DDPs) to ensure the content of the award meets the needs of the vocational sector.

The cornerstone of this programme is the development of functional skills, which is the ability to use English, mathematics and ICT in a range of every-day and work settings. This supports the government's drive for participation in learning of young people to reach a target of 90 per cent by 2015 (Leitch, 2006). To achieve the diploma at Foundation level, learners will have to achieve a Level 1 in functional skills and a Level 2 for the Higher and Advanced diploma. Essential to the learning experience will be the ability to develop and apply knowledge and skills to the sector-related area. Project-based activities are employed, designed to show learning and thinking skills and give the opportunity to practically apply functional skills.

Many of the colleges and training providers achieved a CoVE (Centre of Vocational Excellence) status. This meant that the provider was deemed to offer a high-quality specialist vocational provision, meeting the needs of employers as well as enabling learners from all backgrounds to have the opportunity to access high-quality vocational training, thus helping them to achieve employment. However, CoVE status may be phased out in the next few years.

Diplomas are not intended to be delivered by any one institution and collaboration will be essential. This will include examinations officers maintaining close links as it will need to be decided who will be responsible for registering learners and for ensuring that any necessary access arrangements will be in place. From 2010, the funding streams currently managed by the local authorities and the Learning and Skills Council will come under the sole responsibility of the local authority for learners up to 18 years of age.

Transition at 14

Transition planning for learners is crucial for effective planning of resources and for ensuring that appropriate support is put in place. There are transitional aspects for all learners who move from school to college, but where students with statements of special educational needs are concerned there should be a transition plan in place. This should be prepared by the school during a pupil's Year 9, but it is not yet clear how such transitions will be affected by the increase in college-based Key Stage 4 provision, or by the raising of the school leaving age. Whether or not there is a transition plan, close links with schools and the SENCOs involved are essential for sharing information, with the permission of the learner. This is particularly important since 14-year-old students who are attending the FE college will continue to be on the roll of their designated school.

Information will need to be shared with partner organisations involved in work-related learning (WRL), raising the question of whether WRL providers should be involved in the learners' review of targets. The provider of the WRL should have a member of staff who manages the provision, and links in with the LA and schools. There may not be examinations to complete but there will be a portfolio of work. Learners can use photographs of tasks completed, such as in disassembling a car brake system and putting it back together. This allows them the opportunity to reflect on the sequencing of the task and its health and safety implications, and to cue their thoughts for writing a short piece about the activity in their portfolio. For a learner who experiences dyslexia this could be done by using ICT, or it could be possible to have the support of a teaching assistant who would scribe for the learner. What is important is that dyslexic students can demonstrate knowledge and understanding in ways that suit their learning style.

The demands of a vocational perspective

Young learners following a vocational route will be expected to learn new skills in relation to their chosen study area. They will need to learn the vocational language to be able to concentrate on following verbal instructions, to read technical drawings and to demonstrate skills in hand and eye coordination. Where a student experiences dyslexia, these requirements will then present a new set of challenges. Within work settings it may be difficult for dyslexic trainees or employees to manage their dyslexia difficulties, especially if employers are unaware of their duty to make reasonable adjustments.

A pilot study of SpLD disclosure in the workplace (Martin and McLoughlin, 2008) surveyed a small sample of adults about whether they had disclosed their difficulties in the workplace, and looked at the important factors around this issue. There was a number of reasons given for non-disclosure and for not requesting adjustments, and this perhaps highlights that raising awareness is essential in the workplace for line managers and human resources managers. Reasons for non-disclosure included 'not wanting to stand out', 'no reason, providing the job gets done as it should', and 'they would not understand what dyslexia is all about'. These comments raise the question of how far employers understand their duties under the Disability Discrimination Act.

Work-related learning is now embedded as part of the Key Stage 4 provision. It has been recognised that disaffection and disengagement from education has wider implications for the community and country as a whole. The importance of engaging employers in this programme leads to a greater opportunity of meeting learners' needs. For some learners, a WRL programme will be a preferred educational route to that offered by the school alone.

A way to improve the work-related learning (WRL) experience may be to encourage dyslexic adults to become workplace mentors for young people with dyslexia. Coping strategies for day-to-day activities can be shared and can help change the view that experiencing dyslexia may in some way be a hindrance to achievement. WRL can give young learners the opportunity to learn strategies to deal with real-life challenges, and there is also a learning opportunity for forward-thinking employers in recognising that dyslexic employees can offer skills and benefits and strengths to the workplace.

The debate: are there tensions between the different emphases and expectations in 14+ FE provision?

The FE sector has encompassed a wide range of educational purposes, offering courses ranging from functional social skills modules to degree programmes, but with a central purpose in vocational education. While initiatives following the Leitch report focused on literacy and numeracy targets, the vocational requirement has remained, seeming to place upon FE the responsibility of addressing social, economic and sometimes educational causes for concern. This widest of responsibilities has sometimes given rise to tensions within and between FE providers, and Eccelstone confirms that:

> Staff feel immensely pressurised by the impact of planning, funding, targets, inspection and the endless wave of initiatives. (Ecclestone, 2006: 16)

The reform of 14 + provision in FE provides an infrastructure that is intended to develop both the basic skills purpose and the vocational purpose within FE. Key Stage 4 provision seeks to prepare young people for adult life with skills in literacy, numeracy and ICT, and the inclusion of vocational training prepares students for developing and constructing their career. Skills provision includes the development of social behaviour and communication expected in the workplace. The modern apprenticeship framework continues this theme by featuring key skills subjects as a core part of the qualification framework.

Key technique: flashcards

It is essential that young learners are aware of the boundaries for behaviour in the college environment, which should also reflect expectations in a normal working environment. Flashcards are a good way of reinforcing learning concepts and securing understanding of a topic; for example, health and safety regulations. They promote adaptive behaviour by attracting students' attention, stimulating learning through multisensory input and by alleviating dyslexia stresses associated with more traditional forms of input.

To use flashcards effectively with older learners, we need to ensure that the lesson is well structured, objectives are well defined at the start of the lesson and that learners are aware of boundaries in the workshop environment.

- Flashcards can be useful for carrying out a number of reinforcement activities.
- Matching cards for terms and definitions can be used in revision sessions.
- Complex vocational words can be written on a flashcard and learners can segment the word by using scissors to cut out the relevant parts. The parts can be blended to identify the word and the learner then writes the word in his/her subject glossary.

What does the Code of Practice say about adjustments for all students?

The *Disability Discrimination Act 1995: Code of Practice Post-16*, for obvious reasons, does not specifically address post-14 students. However, it confirms that reasonable adjustments are the duty of all institutions, and this would make a college the provider of last resort for post-14 FE students if there were no other resources available. The Code points out that adjustments are relative to the size of the establishment. Reasonable adjustments are made in addition to what is already available and this means that a large institution, such as a major university, can do more from within existing budgets than can a small college. However the code advises that:

> Even when an education provider's budget has been exhausted, they will still be required to make reasonable adjustments (DRC, 2007: 82, para. 5.42).

 ## Case study: Amelia; a challenging student

Amelia, aged 15, arrived in the college, with a reputation for bad behaviour. There was little recorded information available for her as her family had moved around the country and Amelia had also truanted on many occasions. An old statement of SEN mentioned social, emotional and behavioural difficulties and attention deficit, literacy difficulties and lack of academic progress. Her attitude caused some to view her as troublesome but her tutor, in looking at her work, began to wonder if Amelia might experience dyslexia. However, the tutor also questioned whether her literacy difficulties might be the result of a lack of educational experience. In addition, Amelia had been prescribed Ritalin which would affect her study because, at times of the day when the effect of her medication retreated, her difficulties would increase.

In response to the tutor's concerns, Amelia was referred for a dyslexia assessment, which identified her as experiencing dyslexia. Necessary adjustments were put in place, including specialist tuition, in-class support, extra time and a scribe in examinations.

Unfortunately, these adjustments caused difficulties because Amelia was still of school age and technically on the roll of her local secondary school, even though she had attended only on the day that she was enrolled. The school, without experience of her education, was not in a position to say where among their pupils entitled to SEN funding arrangements she would have been placed, and therefore was not ready to make funding available to support her. Although there was the record of an old statement, this had lapsed and Amelia was not known to the Connexions adviser. Requests went back and forth between the school, college and LA, as agreement was sought about how to provide help for Amelia.

The FE dyslexia specialist comments

Amelia's particular profile of difficulties and her mixed educational history make it unlikely that she is going to have a long concentration span, and at times of the day she may be able to concentrate only for minutes, even seconds. Amelia's subject tutors should be tolerant of distractibility and not see it as a personal challenge.

Practitioners should seek the advice of the SENCO in developing strategies for managing her behaviour; the first priority is to keep Amelia in the learning setting of her own volition. Tutors need to be prepared to offer learning in very small steps, being tolerant if Amelia stops work or fidgets, or if her gaze wanders round the room. Some might advocate deliberately giving her items to fidget with, and rather than criticising her, Amelia could be gently encouraged to put herself back to work after she has become distracted. Her dyslexia must not be overlooked in the attention given to her behaviour.

Amelia is working towards a qualification in the college. Carrying out an assessment would also be useful in identifying her strengths and weaknesses. This can lead to strategies and support being provided to improve Amelia's learning and behaviour. The consistency provided by a stable educational situation may also help. If difficulties persist in arranging an assessment through the LA, then the college has a 'moral obligation' to ensure their student has proper access arrangements in place.

The HE dyslexia specialist comments

If Amelia progressed to HE, she may find that the greater emphasis on being independent in living as well as in her studies is more stressful. As she may have more complex situations to face at university, Amelia may find herself becoming frustrated and possibly aggressive. The specialist support tutor must allow Amelia to express her difficulties at the beginning of a one-to-one session and provide her with strategies to remain calm. A referral to the university counselling service or the Wellbeing Centre may be appropriate.

 Points for discussion

- Overlapping responsibilities can cause confusion. Who has the obligation, or the duty, to assess Amelia – the college, the school, or the local authority?
- How can subject teachers, tutors and lecturers support Amelia in her studies?
- Should Amelia be excluded if she misbehaves and has rows with her tutors?
- Should the college SENCO encourage Amelia's mother to approach the school, college or local authority to seek extra support for Amelia?

In the end, the LA agreed to provide exceptional support funding for Amelia, but insisted that a statutory re-assessment procedure would have to take place, even though Amelia was 15. Once her dyslexia had been identified by the college, and tuition and support were put in place Amelia began to make literacy progress. Her behaviour also modified, although there were still flare-ups. There was once a very bad altercation between tutor and student that almost resulted in her permanent exclusion. However, Amelia was able to maintain her placement and plan her career.

Summary

1   Further education is changing to take into account the provision of Key Stage 4 learning, with a particular emphasis on vocational training. These changes have a social and economic purpose: to ensure that the UK has a highly trained and competent workforce that will compete in the global market.
2   There are learners who do not readily acquire sound literacy skills and issues of resourcing have, in the past, presented difficulties. The achievement of functional skills in literacy, numeracy and ICT remain important in FE provision, driven by the targets set by Lord Leitch.
3   The changes to the National Curriculum and the introduction of vocational diplomas offer new opportunities for Key Stage 4 (post-14) learners. The success of work-related learning and the new diplomas will depend on collaboration between providers and schools.

Further reading

Bartlett, D. and Moody, S. (2004) *Dyslexia in the Workplace*. London: Whurr.

Department for Children, Schools and Families (DCSF) (2008) *The Work-Related Learning Guide*. London: DCSF. Available online at http://publications.teachernet.gov.uk/

Long, R. (2009) *Intervention Toolbox: for Social, Emotional and Behavioural Difficulties*. London: Sage.

Assistive software

The graphic representation at the start of this chapter was completed using Inspiration version 7. This is a commercially available product that has a wide range of templates for academic use. It is regularly used in colleges and may be recommended in a needs assessment for Disabled Students' Allowance in HE.

Student comment

'I think because I went from school to college and on to university, it was perfect and I would advise people to do this. You're treated a lot more adult-like in college; you get the independence; you get the workload and when I came to university the jump didn't seem too great for me ... my transition was the perfect transition because it eases you in slowly between the three different institutional bodies'. Siobhan

Social and emotional aspects of dyslexia-friendly HE and FE

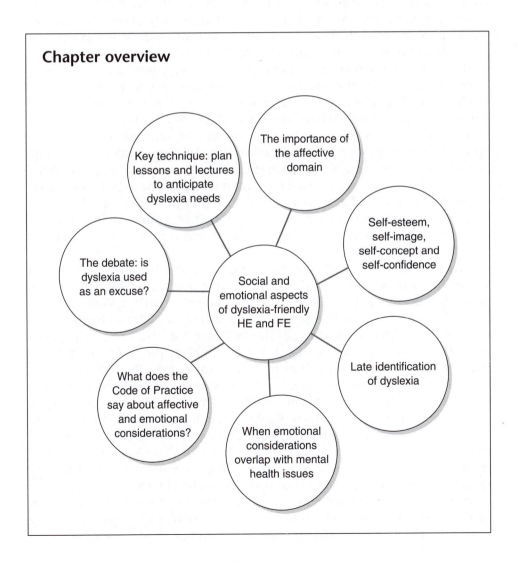

The importance of the affective domain

Current dyslexia literature acknowledges the relevance of emotional and affective factors in seeking to understand the impact of dyslexia upon learners in FE and HE. Pollak (2005) in particular considers the social and emotional domain, focusing upon the life stories of individual students. Emotional/affective factors are more powerful and engaging than cognitive ones, and current approaches to learning consider that the cognitive and affective domains are inextricably linked. Consequently, this chapter has an explicit point to make: that to take care of affective and emotional aspects in learning also enables educators to have access to, and develop, cognitive learning.

Anxiety and stress interfere with learning and this applies to learners who experience dyslexia. Adult learners, particularly those for whom identification has come late in life, may still carry the burden of unhappy school, family or work experiences. Even when they may have apparently developed strategies and come to terms with their own learning difficulties, dyslexic learners may have spent all their educational lives asking themselves repeatedly, 'Why can't I do this?', with all the potential for anxiety that this may provide.

It is certainly the case that all tutors of learners who experience dyslexia will need to allow time to hear their stories and experiences; this is an important part of the learning process for tutors and students alike. The tutor's role is not just to deliver field of study knowledge, but to help learners to take advantage of the learning opportunity by supporting their confidence. This can happen when tutors accept and acknowledge personal stories, taking from them an understanding of students' own perceptions of how they learn best and how they need to be taught. These stories may be revisited more than once, since they are indicators of just how deep and powerful the experience has been. It is no use saying that this should be the domain of counsellors – students may need the lecturer to know what it is like for them.

Often the stories are sadly familiar, consisting of insensitive treatment at school, home or work, assumptions made and opportunities lost. One HE student refers to the sense of loneliness that a person with dyslexia can feel (Gilbride, 2007). Against this can be set the recent attitudinal change resulting from the principled position of disability activists, who reject the judgemental, deficit-based view, and consider themselves proud of the different learning and attitudinal characteristics which may exist alongside, or be part of, their dyslexia. These additional characteristics may provide adult learners with insights, strategies and talents, including the capacity to overcome difficult circumstances. Although as Burden and Burdett (2005: 102) suggest, 'dyslexic pride' may be the next phase of development in dyslexia awareness, this may be the province of more mature learners – it seems less likely that students recently in school, where they have been surrounded by literacy tasks at all times, will embrace this particular point of view with ease.

Today, there is rekindled interest in the affective domain, in its present manifestation as emotional intelligence, made popular through the work of Goleman (1995). It is important then to remember to pay attention to the affective domain, since taking care of the emotional aspects of learning creates a climate of reassurance that allows learning to proceed.

Taking care of the affective aspects of the dyslexia experience does not necessarily mean that a lecturer or tutor must change their demeanour. It does mean, however, that they must develop their pedagogic practice to be aware of the emotional issues and take care to reduce any possible barriers that may result. This can be helped considerably by adopting dyslexia-friendly practices. In an extreme example, one student known to the authors, a person who was a very speedy thinker in all aspects except those of literacy, needed a private agreement that he could leave the lecture room when it all became too much for him. He would sit outside and then go back in when he felt calmer. He graduated with a 2:1.

Self-esteem, self-image, self-concept and self-confidence

In seeking to understand the constructs underpinning a person's sense of self and identity, a number of terms have come into use. Wearmouth, Soler and Reid find it necessary to warn that:

> although the terms self-esteem, self-concept and self-image are sometimes used interchangeably they do have different but interrelated meanings. (Wearmouth, Soler and Reid, 2002: 284)

Against these psychological and research-led constructs, self-confidence is perhaps best seen as a generic, more publicly-used concept. The term implies elements such as self-esteem, self-concept and a sense of efficacy, a belief in one's ability to cope – elements which place matters of self-confidence firmly within the affective domain. Riddick notes the difficulty of clarifying the relationship of self-esteem and academic performance, recommending Lawrence's (1985) view that:

> in the absence of more convincing evidence it's safest to assume that we need to work on both children's self-beliefs and their learning skills. (Riddick, 1996: 37)

Gilroy describes how anxiety can be exacerbated by study difficulties associated with dyslexia. She points out the reliance upon written text within the HE study environment, noticing how 'the student may panic when faced with tasks in which his dyslexia may be exposed' (Gilroy, 2004: 36). In contrast to a lack of output, she notes that an alternative response may be that of overactivity; in the effort to overcome difficulties, students may attempt to do so much that confusion may result, leading to further anxiety.

It may be possible that feelings of reduced academic self-concept or self-worth in young people who experience dyslexia may ameliorate as they become older (Burden, 2008). It is possible too that self-concept may improve as literacy skills improve. However, some people will continue to feel negatively affected by the impact of their dyslexia and, further, the emotional impact of late identification of dyslexia must also be considered. This may present a different, or differently organised, experience.

Late identification of dyslexia

It is not unusual for students to have their dyslexia identified only when they reach the stage of FE or HE. Widening participation and access initiatives are bringing into the colleges and universities, students who do not have a conventional examination-based academic experience. Adult literacy initiatives, access and life-long learning policies also increase the range of educational experience of students. While younger students are more likely to have their dyslexia identified during their school years, this is not always the case. It may not be until students have had difficulty with the programme, assignment or examination that they may seek the advice of the student support service, or that a tutor may suggest a discussion with the service. It may be imagined what thoughts, fears and doubts might go through a student's mind, and what cross-checking and information-gathering they might carry out before they feel able to consult a member of the disability team. This would not be an action taken lightly and it is only the first step.

Confirmation of dyslexia may have an enormous impact upon a learner. While the identification of dyslexia may bring some comfort in providing an explanation, it may then take a lengthy period of time, perhaps years, to come to terms with it. With the identification of dyslexia an entire change of self-perception may be necessary. Further, the identification of dyslexia means that learners may have to take on a whole new body of knowledge about dyslexia and integrate it into both their self-perception and their learning routines. Where identification comes late, this may take place mid-programme, and entail a struggle to adjust which is often overlooked. A student may not auto-matically understand the characteristics of dyslexia or which facets of their own learning style are the consequences of dyslexia. They may not make allowances for their own learning differences or know how best they might be helped.

The reaction of family and friends may be a further factor. Responses may range from denial of the existence of a real condition called dyslexia, to puzzle-ment and uncertain reactions from people who were close and thought they knew the learner, to bitterness, as Scott (2003) points out, when others have struggled without help or opportunity. Entire re-calibration of family and friends' understanding of a student's identity, and the re-evaluation of past events and experiences, may be required. Dyslexia-friendly practice recognises the emotional and affective factors involved.

When emotional considerations overlap with mental health issues

A student may be stressed and/or angry, not just re-evaluating, if they have been assessed recently for dyslexia. Emotional 'backwash' may affect wider aspects of a student's life, just as external emotional situations may have an exacerbating impact upon a student's dyslexia, with the potential for the impact in either direction to be extreme. For most professionals this is most likely to be manifest as non-coping behaviour that affects the submission or quality of assignments, rather than anything more worrying. However, it is helpful to be alert to possible situations that contribute to stress, and often these will be academic related.

If a student has fragile self-esteem, they may take criticism personally and negatively. If a student is upset about an essay mark or comment, sometimes the effect can be reduced by pointing out that it may not have been meant in the way it was taken. Tutors can help by framing marks or comments in such a way as to praise the student for the assignment's strengths, but to criticise the assignment when discussing weaknesses and covering the strengths first. Comments can include targets for improvement that would, if followed judiciously, help a student to move their marks up the marking band, or into the next band, rather than aiming at an ultimate, full-flowering meeting of the highest criteria. It is also helpful if tutors are willing to discuss their feedback comments.

A serious concern for many professionals in FE and HE is the point where emotional cosiderations seem so extreme as to be viewed as mental health issues. These may result in alarming behaviour and it is possible that some students with dyslexia would occasionally fall into this group. A specialist tutor would be able to check a student's file to see if he or she is already seeing the counselling service or the mental health coordinator (MHC). However, for a subject or progress/personal tutor to raise the question of counselling with a dyslexic learner is a matter of great sensitivity and one which many might feel reluctant to undertake. In a college there will be a special educational needs coordinator (SENCO) who can advise. Although in a university setting a lecturer can turn to the disability support team for advice, he or she may well be the one to suggest to the student that they approach the counselling service. However in pursuing this route there is also an ethical dimension to consider, concerning intrusion into the private concerns of individuals.

It is up to the student to decide whether he or she wishes to attend counselling, and for most FE and HE students who experience dyslexia, emotional and affective aspects of their learning will be managed by themselves with or without the help of counsellors. However, in extreme cases, a student's difficulties may become so severe that they are better described as mental health difficulties. Colleges and universities have a mental health coordinator who liaises with staff, student services, mental health services, GPs and students. A subject, personal/progress or specialist tutor may wish to keep in touch with the MHC, but will not always be told the details of what the MHC discusses.

It is worrying to some professionals that students with difficulties of this magnitude are part of the FE and HE world, but there are important points to consider. First, they are part of everybody's world of work; the days of excluding members of society who do not fit in with restrictive norms are over. Second, mental health problems are recognised as a disability under the terms of the 2001 Special Educational Needs and Disability Act, itself amending the Disability Discrimination Act 1995. This means that where difficulties are severe and long-standing, they are regarded as a disability and must be treated as such. This also means that a student cannot be refused admission or excluded on the grounds of their disability. Reasonable adjustments must be made and it is only when such adjustments are thought to be 'unreasonable' that difficulties of this kind would become grounds for refusal or exclusion.

The debate: is dyslexia used as an excuse?

It is possible to encounter the idea of dyslexia being used as an excuse to gain advantages, such as extra time, or sympathetic marking, or resources such as computers and software. Several factors may contribute to such perceptions, which may themselves rest on a limited understanding of dyslexia. It may seem to some that dyslexia means an inability to read, or consistent letter reversal, so that a dyslexic student who can read or produce reasonable work, may be accused of faking. This may reinforce, and be reinforced by, a belief that there is 'no such thing' as dyslexia, possibly being an invention of middle class parents to account for their children's scholastic difficulties. The issue of whether support should be given to students who experience only mild dyslexia also remains in question. The fact is that the literacy demands of HE make it likely that most of the dyslexic students in HE will experience dyslexia in its mild to moderate form, so they will not manifest the more severe characteristics of dyslexia identified in the public perception; the impact of dyslexia may not be immediately apparent. In FE, more severe ranges of dyslexia may be found, but then dyslexia issues may become tangled up with school failure, perceived as lack of effort. Further, some-one whose dyslexia has been identified by comparison with their higher level of ability in other areas, so that their literacy skills appear to be at a level similar to a non-dyslexic peer, may be accused of 'pretending'.

The reality is that it would probably not be possible to pretend, convincingly, to have dyslexia in order to gain advantage or resources. The assessment process includes a range of protocols and procedures, some of which focus upon aspects of dyslexia that would not be apparent to someone who did not experience them in real life. Harrison, Edwards and Parker (2008) carried out research into whether students without dyslexia could feign the disability under assessment conditions. One of their findings was that the feigning group read more slowly than the slowest dyslexic student! In addition to this, the persistence of a stu-dent's dyslexia characteristics over time and a student's account of the impact of dyslexia upon their life experiences, including those aspects concerned with confidence and self-esteem, would make faking difficult to sustain.

Key technique: plan lessons and lectures to anticipate dyslexia needs

The dyslexia-friendly lesson or lecture plan shown in Appendix 5 has its ori-gins in a model by Hillier (2002). It is designed for group or class use, but it can also be used for individual students. The lecture plan includes a checklist of dyslexia-friendly pedagogical characteristics and a reminder of important study-related skills. Planning a lecture or session in this way maximises the opportunity to anticipate the learning needs of dyslexic students. Planned accommodations for someone who experiences mental health difficulties can be added, in discreet terms, as individual access arrangements.

What does the Code of Practice say about affective and emotional considerations?

While the Code of Practice might seem to focus on the more apparent aspects of disability, it is sufficiently flexible to address emotional and affective considerations also. The *Disability Discrimination Act 1995: Code of Practice Post-16* (DRC, 2007) makes the point that, among people who experience disabilities:

> The nature and extent of their disabilities vary widely, as do their requirements for overcoming any difficulties which they may face. If education providers are to avoid discriminating, they need to understand this, and to be aware of the effects that their decisions and actions – and those of their agents and employees – may have on disabled people. (DRC, 2007: 15, para. 2.4)

 ### Case study: Loni; tutor time lost in tears

Loni, aged 60, was a mature student. Following an Access course, Loni went through the referral and assessment process, receiving help from the local authority which included individual tuition from a specialist tutor. However, the tutor was dismayed to find that on every occasion that Loni came to her support lesson, she would, after a while, become distressed, and this would quickly turn to tears. The tutor felt as if the session was being washed away in a flood. Loni's distress was related not just to her present difficulties and her past educational experience. Early in each lesson her thoughts would turn inevitably to a much-loved grandmother, now deceased, who had brought her up. If asked why she was distressed, Loni would say, 'If Nana could see me now ...', but nothing further. It was difficult to proceed with the lesson after that.

The FE dyslexia specialist comments

There are clearly unresolved issues for Loni that can be dealt with only by a counsellor. It is important to recognise that as a specialist tutor our skills are in supporting Loni and to give her strategies to cope with her learning and develop her underpinning skills. It is common that adult learners will use the session to talk about personal matters; this reflects the trust that the one-to-one

(Continued)

(Continued)

relationship brings. A discussion with Loni's progress/personal tutor would also help to identify if this has arisen on other occasions or with other staff. Loni's support sessions should start with a clear set of objectives to be achieved by the end of the session, and in a gentle but firm way the lesson plan should be worked through. Within the lesson plan Loni should be allowed five minutes, certainly no more than 10, to reflect on her coursework and to express how she feels she is progressing. It will help if she can identify the successes that she has had, in feedback from course tutors, such as a well-planned and constructed piece of work or being able to carry out independent research for a particular topic.

Her grandmother was clearly a big influence in her life and no doubt would have expressed pride in her granddaughter's achievements. Loni should be able to reflect on this and feel positive about her progress. Close contact should be maintained with the progress/personal tutor to ensure Loni is supported by all to achieve a pass on her course.

The HE dyslexia specialist comments

At the first session the tutor could suggest to Loni that her obvious distress was making such an impact on her studies that she might receive considerable relief from talking to a counsellor. The tutor could give an outline of the service, stressing confidentiality and that they have a counsellor who has a particular insight into dyslexia. Before the next meeting with Loni the tutor could ask the mental health coordinator if she would be able to see Loni and explain the university's stress management pack and cassette to her. If Loni did not improve the tutor could suggest she see the mental health coordinator about stress management and might also suggest various relaxation methods. The tutor could monitor Loni's stress levels at each session. He or she could let her talk for around a maximum of 10 minutes then remind her, gently, that a tutor is not a counsellor and the session is about study skills tuition. But the tutor would offer all services if it seemed appropriate.

〰 Points for discussion

- Should the support tutor contact the other tutors or lecturers and tell them about Loni's distress, or is this a private matter for Loni?
- If the other tutors know about Loni's distress, should they amend the programme content or delivery in any way? If so, how?
- Should her personal/progress tutor talk to Loni about her dyslexia or about her emotional reaction?
- Should Loni have been accepted onto the programme?

The outcome was that the support tutor continued with the sessions and Loni continued to attend. The support tutor left it to Loni to inform her other tutors and she chose not to do so. However, during her first year, Loni received a learning support agreement, which told tutors how to help her in lectures. Gradually the situation improved as Loni learned new study habits and increased in confidence, and she gained pass grades for her assignments.

 ## Summary

1 Affective/emotional aspects and cognitive aspects of functioning are inextricably linked.
2 It is important to take care of the affective/emotional elements in the learning of dyslexic (and other) students. Anxiety almost certainly makes learning harder, so a tutor or lecturer who reduces the risk of anxiety helps learners towards successful outcomes.
3 The days of considering that students do not belong in the academy when they experience dyslexia or other individual learning characteristics are over. Supporting students' self-confidence through dyslexia-friendly practice can bring about powerful results for students and tutors.

Further reading

Burden, B. (2008) 'Is dyslexia necessarily associated with negative feelings of self-worth? A review and implications for further research', *Dyslexia*, 14: 188–96.

Dale, M. and Taylor, B. (2001) 'How adult learners make sense of their dyslexia', *Disability and Society*, 16 (7): 997–1008.

Miles, T. (ed.) (2004) *Dyslexia and Stress* (second edition). London: Whurr.

Assistive software

The graphical representation at the start of this chapter is provided through the use of Vista software in the standard Microsoft 2007 installation package. It is found by going to the 'insert' menu, then choosing 'SmartArt' on the 'insert' toolbar.

Student comment

'It was put down to laziness I think. I wouldn't say I was a lazy person. Some teachers said, "He'll grow out of this problem as he gets older". I think laziness was inferred at my A-levels. He worded it more perhaps, "You should be more careful in your use of language". but I think there is a difference between being careful and needing help maybe, though I'm not an expert'. Arron

National and international perspectives

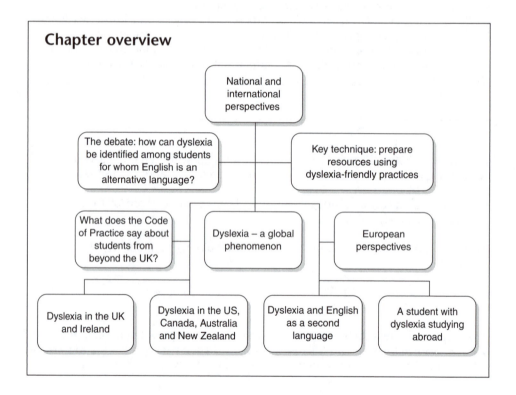

Chapter overview

- National and international perspectives
  - The debate: how can dyslexia be identified among students for whom English is an alternative language?
  - Key technique: prepare resources using dyslexia-friendly practices
  - What does the Code of Practice say about students from beyond the UK?
  - Dyslexia – a global phenomenon
  - European perspectives
    - Dyslexia in the UK and Ireland
    - Dyslexia in the US, Canada, Australia and New Zealand
    - Dyslexia and English as a second language
    - A student with dyslexia studying abroad

Dyslexia – a global phenomenon

Much of the dyslexia literature, and therefore much of what is known about dyslexia, originates in English-speaking contexts. However, the increasing awareness of dyslexia across different countries, encompassing a range of literacy cultures and orthographies, means that dyslexia research now has an international focus. As evidence appears from other languages and orthographies, it appears that dyslexia is manifest in those contexts, but with different emphases. Literature acquisition is still arduous even when there is a close relationship between the sound and the written form of words and word elements. Hypotheses concerned with the speed of processing or memory become more prominent in these shallow orthographies, as this is where the literacy difficulties are more clearly expressed.

Dyslexia in the UK and Ireland

In the UK's home countries of England, Scotland, Wales and Northern Ireland, and Ireland education policy has been decentralised and diversified. The revitalisation of traditional native languages has added a further factor, giving rise to issues concerned with bilingualism and with English as an alternative language.

Scotland

The Scottish government in collaboration with Dyslexia Scotland and others have produced a working definition of dyslexia, providing guidance for all in identifying the indicators and characteristics of dyslexia (Dyslexia Scotland, 2006). This definition makes the point that dyslexia is not linked to cultural or socio-economic backgrounds and recognises that a person will remain with the condition for life. The definition covers the range of difficulties likely to be faced by those experiencing dyslexia, including auditory and visual processing, phonological awareness, short-term working memory and difficulties in being able to carry out organisational skills.

Her Majesty's Inspectorate of Education (HMIE), responsible for ensuring the quality of provision in Scotland's education system, produced *Education for Learners with Dyslexia* (HMIE, 2008). This was a comprehensive review of the whole education system from schools to colleges and universities. The report identified many strengths including the use of multisensory teaching strategies, the use of assistive technologies, and the existence of staff who have the knowledge and experience to ensure identification and assessment of dyslexia at the earliest opportunity. However, many authorities were not able to provide numbers of staff who had gained appropriate specialist qualifications, indicating a pool of unacknowledged expertise. The situation with colleges showed that identification of learners with dyslexia was good, although the colleges felt that more learners should be identified earlier in the school system. The report discussed teacher training in universities and found that there needed to be more time allowed for trainee teachers to be able to fully understand and be confident in identifying and supporting young learners. Time was also needed for students to learn a range of intervention strategies and to become aware of other difficulties associated with dyslexia.

The report concluded that while there is much good practice, there is still room for development and improvement. Professional development for teachers and the sharing of good practice among authorities were seen to be essential.

Wales

Wales is a bilingual country and according to the Welsh Language Board's census in 2001, 37.7 per cent of children between 3 and 15 years speak Welsh. Almost 580,000 people speak Welsh as their first language. The SEN Code of Practice for Wales (Welsh Assembly Government, 2002) allows children to be assessed in Welsh or English in accordance with the 1993 Welsh Language Act, although this is not the case in higher education. In Welsh universities, with the exception of Welsh language studies, Welsh speaking students do not receive tuition in their first language. However, there are a number of FE colleges where Welsh is the first language.

The Welsh Dyslexia Project, which was presented to the National Assembly in 2000, set out to make Wales the best country in which to be an individual with dyslexia. Bilingual resources are available including a version of the adult dyslexia checklist (the English version of this is available on the BDA website) as well as software in the Welsh language. In conjunction with other European partners, the project has explored ICT packages and the support that is available for students in HE institutions.

Ireland and Northern Ireland

The Equal Status Act 2000–2004 requires educational establishments in Ireland to provide reasonable accommodations to students with disabilities, if without such special treatment or facilities it would be impossible or unduly difficult for the person to study. Such accommodation may be refused only if the institution would incur more than nominal cost. In addition, the Employment Equality Act 1998–2004 considers that reasonable accommodations should be applied to students with disabilities in vocational training unless such accommodations give rise to a disproportionate burden (for example, the scale of financial outlay). This Act judges a person who has a disability to be fully competent to undertake, and fully capable of undertaking, any duties provided the necessary accommodations are put in place.

The Student Support Bill 2008 seeks to establish a single unified grant system for students, and disability may be a criterion considered when awarding funds. However, a fund for students with disabilities which is not means tested is provided by the European Social Fund and the Irish Government. The Institution applies for the fund on behalf of the student. Funding is granted only on receipt of a Needs Assessment accompanied by formal documentation identifying a SpLD (i.e. an Educational Psychologist's Report that is no older than five years, although this may change to three years).

In Ireland, the term for post-compulsory education is the Third Level. Students applying to Third Level institutions do so through the Central Applications

Office (CAO) and are invited to disclose a disability, but are not obliged to do so. In 2008, 68,809 students applied through the CAO of which 238 (3.46 per cent) disclosed a disability with 72% of these applicants experiencing SpLDs as their primary disability. 99 per cent of the applicants with SpLDs were students with dyslexia. If a student discloses a disability, the institution is able to contact the student and put support in place.

Students need to meet the Minimum Entry Requirements determined by the institution's admissions policy and any further requirements demanded by the course they intend to pursue. Ireland is, to some extent, bilingual and in the last Census (2006) 40.8 per cent (1,656,790) of the population aged three years and over were equally fluent in English and Irish. There are 139 primary and 39 secondary schools which teach through the medium of Irish (Gaeilscoileanna) in the Irish Republic and 31 primary and 4 secondary Gaeilscoileanna schools in Northern Ireland. Exemptions from the modern language requirement are possible for students with significant learning difficulties. These are gained by applying to the National Union of Ireland, sending evidence such as an educational psychologist's assessment and an exemption from Irish granted by the Department of Education and Science.

Not all Third Level Institutions have a disability officer, but all universities and larger institutes of technology have a dedicated disability service which acts as an advocate for disabled students, mediating in the administration involved in registration or examinations, as well as coordinating educational support (such as note-taker, reader in examinations, material in other formats, specialist tuition, etc.) and general guidance.

In Northern Ireland, further and higher education is the province of the Department for Employment and Learning (DEL) and the system is the same as that in England, with GCSEs and A levels. Colaiste Feirste, set up by the Department of Education to promote education through the medium of Irish, has started A level and vocational type courses in Belfast through Irish for post-16 students (see www.comhairle.org/english/index.php). The Special Educational Needs and Disability Order (SENDO) was passed in 2005 and, like SENDA in the UK, requires institutions not to treat any student less favourably because of their disability, and to make reasonable adjustments.

European perspectives

Across Europe legislation and provision for students with dyslexia studying at university is not consistent. Research carried out for a European Minerva Project and edited by Ian Smythe (2005) is of particular interest. In some countries such as Denmark, Spain and Sweden, dyslexia is formally recognised as a disability, whereas in Austria, France, Poland and Romania it is not. Assessment can be by a psychologist, teacher, speech therapist or GP.

Very few countries provide funding for students with dyslexia either for an assessment as an adult or to pursue a university course, and only then if they experience severe dyslexia. Support in the form of specialist tuition is rarely available, although extra subject-specific tuition may be provided in rare instances. The same can be said of ICT; little specialist software is available, although Sweden does provide talking books. In terms of accommodations for examinations, very little is offered. Extra time may be offered in Spain, and in Poland and Sweden computers may be used. In some countries, for example in Hungary, students must pass an intermediate foreign language examination or they cannot get a place at university. Consequently, only students who can gain entrance places and therefore may have mild dyslexia are likely to be awarded degrees.

A European-funded TEMPUS project for the Identification and Support in Higher Education for Dyslexic Students (ISHEDS) began in 2009 coordinated by Professor Angela Fawcett of Swansea University and Dr Ian Smythe, involving partners in Bosnia-Herzegovina, Croatia, Hungary, Serbia and Slovenia. The two-year project sets out to address inequalities of provision for university students in the Western Balkan higher education systems. The project aims to make an impact on policy and legislation, focusing on Bosnia-Herzegovina, Hungary, Romania and Serbia, as countries that lack laws or guidelines or support for children or adults who experience dyslexia. Assessment of dyslexia, ICT support, human support and self-support for students with dyslexia studying at university are also aspects of the project.

Dyslexia in the US, Canada, Australia and New Zealand

The US, Canada, Australia and New Zealand have a linguistic kinship through the use of English. However, their approaches to dyslexia differ, since Australia and New Zealand do not recognise dyslexia formally. In Canada and the US dyslexia is recognised as a reading disability although the precise definition differs from state to state. In Canada not all universities can provide appropriate support for students with dyslexia, although computers may be allowed in examinations. Both in Canada and the US assessment is private, undertaken by a psychologist, and the format must agree with the requirements of the Association on Higher Education and Disability (AHEAD), a North American organisation. In some cases students may have to finance their own support.

Klassen, Neufeld and Munro (2005) discuss the background to the Australian dyslexia experience and compare it with that of the US. The authors describe how the understanding of learning difficulty is moving away from the use of IQ and discrepancy-based definitions in both the US and Australia. Here the approach to specific learning difficulty in literacy, most frequently described as learning difficulty or learning disability (LD), does not now distinguish dyslexia as a distinct learning characteristic, although this has been the case in the past. Instead the rationale for additional support is based on low achievement, although within this the existence of specific learning difficulties is recognised. There are familiar arguments about whether or not the use of the term 'dyslexia' is helpful, with some people, particularly parents and teachers, regarding this as positive, while others consider that 'labels' are irrelevant and not necessarily helpful in planning appropriate interventions. A perspective of difficulty rather than disability rules the guiding policy. Dyslexia is not formally recognised in New Zealand and, as in Australia, a non-categorical approach prevails.

This brings into focus the issue of how one can have dyslexia-friendly approaches without an acknowledgement of dyslexia. A solution may be found in the application of the principles of Universal Design. This movement originated in the US in the work of Ron Mace, who cross-referenced architectural principles with those of accessibility for disabled people (Center for Universal Design, 1997, cited by Zeff, 2007). This has since resulted in applications in the form of Universal Instructional Design (UID), that extend into non-disabled and neurotypical communities in the same way that dyslexia-friendly principles are expected to.

A student with dyslexia studying abroad

As part of their course of study, UK students with dyslexia may spend a year abroad. European institutions may be involved in the Erasmus programme whereby students are welcomed from participating universities. Students with dyslexia may discuss what sort of adjustments may be available in the host university with their home case workers, who may have links with other universities. Case workers can advise students where the best provision may be found for their difficulties, but they will be directed to the Erasmus coordinator and the host institution once this has been decided.

The Erasmus coordinator carries out all the administrative arrangements in the host institution, ensuring that the student's needs are met. The support available abroad depends on the host institution and may be very different from that provided in the UK. Most institutions participating in the Erasmus programme will offer extra time, a reader or, if necessary, a scribe, but not all offer specialist tuition. In the US the support offered for visiting students varies from state to state.

The Disabled Students' Allowance (DSA) may cover some of the cost of support abroad, so students should contact the LA and make enquiries, as the funding from each LA is different. If the DSA does not cover a student's needs abroad, students with severe disabilities or exceptional special needs may be entitled to have the extra costs of their Erasmus placement covered. Sometimes a student may have to pay for the provision in the first instance and then reclaim the costs later.

Dyslexia and English as an additional language

For an individual learner, dyslexia may be manifest in different ways in different languages. This gives rise to the question as to whether it may be possible for dyslexia to appear present in one language and not another. Since different languages and orthographies have varying underlying structures, it may indeed seem that this is the case. However, there are factors that complicate matters, such as learners' knowledge and expectation of the structures of the new language; the fact that learners may have developed compensatory strategies in their native language; the possible variation in the manifestation of dyslexia in different languages; and the fact that dyslexia difficulties fall within a range. Research continues, reflecting the global importance of literacy and the international interest in improving literacy skills.

Miller-Guron and Lundeberg focused upon a group of young Swedish adults who experienced dyslexia, but who preferred to read in English, a language with a deeper orthography than their own. The authors concluded that there were a number of factors governing this characteristic, including social and environmental as well as cognitive ones. They issue a warning that is of particular relevance for practitioners:

> The common assumption that native language deficits will almost certainly result in failure to read a foreign language can lead to negligence in L2 reading instruction or even an active and deliberate reduction in L2 teaching resources for dyslexic pupils. (Miller-Guron and Lundeberg, 2000: 59–60)

In FE and HE it is important to bear this point in mind. Dyslexia-friendly methods, rather than negative assumptions, should guide second language study provision.

In spite of its orthographic difficulties, English is the medium of education in several countries or is strongly promoted as an alternative language. English is also an international medium of education for study at post-16 level, and programmes in English are offered at HE institutions in other countries across Europe and the rest of the world. With the rationalisation of pan-European levels of tertiary study in line with the Bologna declaration (QAA, 2008), the stage is set for more student movement across countries and continents.

Some students who take up higher level study in the UK will experience unidentified dyslexia. Under SENDA 2001 international students have the same rights as home students to have their learning needs recognised and supported, and adjustments made. International students from non-English speaking countries who come to study in UK colleges and universities, and who have already been identified as experiencing dyslexia, must ensure that the evidence of their disability is translated into English. They may apply to the Financial Contingency Fund for accommodations, but this is means tested. In some universities a portion of the international fund is set aside for dyslexic students.

The debate: how can dyslexia be identified among students for whom English is an alternative language?

This is a growing issue in further education as refugees and migrant workers join courses at their local colleges. A specialist teacher has insufficient knowledge of other languages and will rely on talking to colleagues in the EAL (English as an

Alternative Language) team for advice on orthography and language structure of native languages. In considering dyslexia, it may also be the case that the opportunity of education in the student's developing years was not available or may have been disrupted. Therefore, the length of time that a learner has been a student of English should be considered. For entry to HE, proof is required of passing an English language examination to a prescribed level. However it is still the case that a student may experience unidentified dyslexia.

Smythe (2004) provides useful guidance about how to assess multilingual learners who might experience dyslexia, taking a profiling approach. Some formal assessment materials are available in different language formats. However, it would be difficult for English-speaking assessors to execute these and fluent language speakers who were skilled to carry out the assessments could be hard to find.

Key technique: prepare resources using dyslexia-friendly practices

The resource guidelines forming Part A of the audit tool in Appendix 2 provide an optimum learning experience when paper resources are in use. Practitioners often make their own resources, worksheets and handouts for a particular purpose, but may not know how to make them accessible and dyslexia-friendly. Examples can be found where the copy can be cramped, unclear, possibly handwritten, over-copied or with the print running over the edge of the page. This creates unnecessary barriers to learning, yet failure to understand the resources becomes criticism of students rather than of the resource makers. Making resources as clear as possible will benefit students whose first language is not English, especially when they experience dyslexia.

What does the Code of Practice say about students from beyond the UK?

The *Disability Discrimination Act 1995: Code of Practice Post-16* is clear that the duty not to discriminate against people with disabilities extends to students from outside the UK. It states that:

> the Act applies to any disabled people (including those overseas) who are enquiring about, or applying for, admission to a course in Great Britain, and any disabled students (including those overseas) attending, undertaking, or enrolled upon a course in Great Britain. (DRC, 2007: 35, para. 3.11)

In addition, the student does not have to be taking a complete course to be eligible under the Act.

Case study: Fredy; a man of many languages

Fredy, aged 37, had a varied background and spoke of determination and inventiveness in surviving a range of very difficult situations. By dint of hard work and his impressive ability in a particular subject area he had entered the UK education setting. His tutors considered that he could make a valuable contribution to his subject area and be a skilled practitioner, but that he was gravely hampered by his difficulties in written expression. Fredy had at one point been a refugee and had moved from the country of his birth, where he spoke his native language, to a country in Europe, where he had learned a second language and gained citizenship. Fredy liked to keep reading in this second language, although it was a slow process for him, because he wanted to maintain his skill. English presented him with a third language, and although he could maintain a generally useful level of ability in this, his written language difficulty was beginning to give rise to questions about whether Fredy could manage the course, or whether he might experience dyslexia.

The FE dyslexia specialist comments

A structured support programme initially would establish if Fredy is able to remember spellings that are relevant to his course of study and are required as part of the job knowledge that makes him a skilled practitioner. Also this would demonstrate that he is able to read and understand vocational material after support. If there are still difficulties after this I would recommend an assessment.

We would need background information on Fredy's abilities, as we would with any assessment. It would help to ascertain if there are difficulties in the writing and reading comprehension of his home language, in addition to difficulties with working memory, sequencing difficulties and visual–motor difficulties. An assessment using the Wide Range Intelligence Test (WRIT), (Glutting, Adams and Sheslow, 2000), would give an indication of his non-verbal ability, but it is important to ensure that Fredy understands fully the instructions and the function of the test material. An assessment of phonological awareness would identify whether he was able to carry out a sound–symbol translation. For helping Fredy to understand the instructions or for translating the assessment into his home language, the luxury of access to a translator is unlikely to be available.

The HE dyslexia specialist comments

An assessment by an educational psychologist or appropriate assessor would be the first priority. However, some educational psychologists may not assess someone whose first language is not English, because of the potential for misunderstanding and because norms for standardised tests are generally based on the responses of native English speakers. In such a case we would have to search for an assessor who spoke Fredy's first language, or seek a bilingualism specialist. The library would arrange the loan of IT equipment in the form of recording devices and laptops but we would need to seek funding to pay for person-based support such as tuition or note-taking. This might possibly be available from the international students contingency fund. Another possibility is that if Fredy has lived for six months in any one area, the LA might support him – but he would have to have been resident in the UK for at least three years. In terms of specialist support, written work and grammar would be the main areas on which to focus.

〰️ Points for discussion

1 What is more important for Fredy – diagnostic assessment for dyslexia or strategies to help him to improve his use of the English language?
2 Is it appropriate to tell Fredy that he should be using the English language more often?
3 What could the teacher, tutor or lecturer do in the learning setting to help Fredy to master his subject-specific vocabulary?
4 Should Fredy be encouraged to intercalate (take a year out) while he improves his contextual knowledge of the English language?

Fredy was assessed by the student support service and it was felt that he showed dyslexic tendencies. However, this was not seen as a secure identification because of the complications presented by his interrupted educational background and the confusions in his use of language. It was considered that Fredy would benefit from additional dyslexia-based support lessons and discussion took place as to how this should be funded. However, it was pointed out that the terms of SENDA 2001 applied to everyone studying in the country and that the college had to therefore be the provider, if there was no other. Fredy was diligent in his attendance at the support sessions and with the help of the tutor developed techniques for remembering his English subject vocabulary. His progress in written work was slow, but with hard work and persistence he was able to keep pace with his programme.

Summary

1 Dyslexia is a global phenomenon, but it may be expressed differently within different orthographies.
2 Since the expression of dyslexia is affected by language and orthography, it may be the case that a student displays difficulties in one language but not another, or at least displays them more severely in one language than in another.
3 Dyslexia within varying language contexts is a research topic of considerable global interest and activity at the present time, and may add new perspectives to the way that dyslexia is viewed.

Further reading 📖

Peer, L. and Reid, G. (eds) (2000) *Multilingualism, Literacy and Dyslexia: A Challenge for Educators*. London: David Fulton.

Smythe, I., Everatt, J. and Salter, R. (eds) (2004) *International Book of Dyslexia: A Cross-Language Comparison and Practice Guide.* Chichester: Wiley.

Sunderland, H., Klein, C., Savinson, R. and Partridge, T. (1997) *Dyslexia and the Bilingual Learner.* Stevenage: Avanti Books.

Assistive software

The graphical representation at the start of this chapter was created by using an organisation chart in Microsoft Word. This is accessed by choosing 'insert' from the toolbar, selecting 'diagram' and then selecting a chart, which can be a choice of Venn, pyramid, cycle, target and radial diagrams.

Student comment

'The department were excellent and really helpful. When I was growing up I started reading in English, and in exams it used to take me a long time to the read the paper and everyone else would have started writing perhaps a whole page and that would make me panic, but once I had extra time it was certainly a great help and took the pressure off me'. Marie

Dyslexia and disability-friendly perspectives

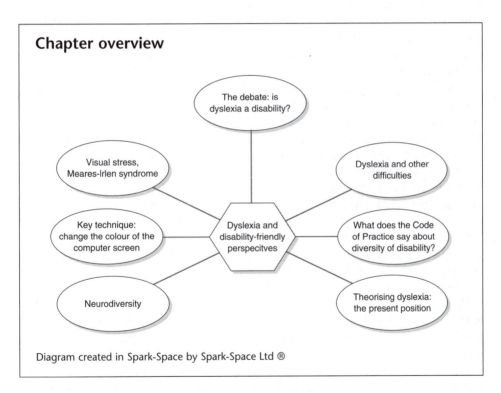

Chapter overview

- The debate: is dyslexia a disability?
- Visual stress, Meares-Irlen syndrome
- Dyslexia and other difficulties
- Key technique: change the colour of the computer screen
- Dyslexia and disability-friendly perspecitves
- What does the Code of Practice say about diversity of disability?
- Neurodiversity
- Theorising dyslexia: the present position

Diagram created in Spark-Space by Spark-Space Ltd ®

Theorising dyslexia: the present position

Dyslexia hypotheses are generally based on a perception of individual deficit and take a medical or psychological focus. This is a view of dyslexia that locates it within symbolic learning, that is, something that happens in the brain, rather than situated learning, which happens in social settings. However, the well-known Morton and Frith model (Morton and Frith, 1995, cited in Frith, 1999) includes an environmental dimension running alongside the cognitive, biological and behavioural levels, so that in every dyslexia hypothesis there is an environmental aspect. It is this that the dyslexia-friendly initiative addresses, on the understanding that by improving the learning environment, the chances of successful learning can be improved. Currently, many researchers seek for an understanding of the genes that may be implicated, recognising heritability in dyslexia. It has become apparent that there is no single 'dyslexia gene' but rather a number of genes are involved, with some attention being drawn to KIAA0319 on chromosome 6p22. Paracchini et al. (2008) describe this as the 'dyslexia susceptibility gene' but note also that it influences general reading ability.

Dyslexia specialists and researchers have put great effort into establishing the validity of the concept of dyslexia, locating it in differences in the brain, but also recognising the impact of the learning setting and the characteristics of teaching. For the last 30 years there has been strong support for the phonological deficit or difference as the core characteristic of dyslexia. The phonological deficit theory posits that dyslexic difficulties have their origin in the language centres of the brain, and that dyslexia is effectively an inability to match spoken sounds (phonemes) with the written versions of the same sounds (graphemes), so that reading and spelling consistency are extremely difficult to establish and retain.

Others have felt that the phonological deficit theory did not account for all the characteristics associated with dyslexia. Key theories in the dyslexia debate were outlined by Angela Fawcett in her review for the Department for Education and Skills and two major UK dyslexia organisations (Fawcett 2001). In addition to the phonological theory, represented by a large body of research in which the work of Margaret Snowling and the York group is predominant, Fawcett's review included, among others, the Cerebellar theory, covering the possible impact of skills fluency, automaticity and motor skills in the gaining of literacy (Nicholson and Fawcett 1999); the Magnocellular theory (Stein 2001), covering the timing of visual effects in reading, and the 'double deficit theory' (Wolf and Bowers, 1999), which is concerned with phonological processing, together with the speed of processing.

These are all explanatory causal theories, and they have been concurrent with the interpretive 'dual route' theory of Castles and Coltheart (1993), which argues that learning to read takes place on a lexical or whole-word level, and on a sub-lexical, word-building level that helps readers to interpret words and clusters of sounds not seen before. However, the discussion of dyslexia theories is currently changing as evidence accumulates from other languages, from genetic research and from brain imaging studies. An example can be found in the work of Zeigler et al., (2003) who, in considering alternative orthographies, found that there was common ground in the slow speed of processing of phonological components, thereby relating phonological deficit to temporal processing.

Dyslexia theory may be in a time of paradigm change, bearing in mind that understanding of dyslexia is bound up with how it is defined and assessed. Nevertheless, debate may be moving away from looking for the culprit characteristic in the brain and moving towards theories which consider as neurological interconnectedness as part of the phenomenon of dyslexia. This current interest includes both cognitive and biological connection; there is also an interest in neuroplasticity, which refers to the capacity of the brain to change as a result of experience. These perspectives have their origins in earlier theoretical constructs, reconsidered in the light of currently developing understanding, and include:

- renewed interest in the connectionist account (see, for example, Griffiths and Snowling 2002; Ziegler and Goswami, 2005) which considers interconnected networks in the brain
- continued interest in the role of memory, with a new focus on declarative and procedural memory (Ullman, 2004, cited in Nicholson and Fawcett, 2008); impairment in procedural memory, which is the memory for skills, is believed to have an impact on lexical and grammatical skills
- a further focus on the role of auditory and visual automatic attention as an innate cognitive process in the gaining of literacy skills, related to temporal processing and compromised in the instance of dyslexia (Facoetti et al., 2003)
- a development of the speed of processing theory in the form of asynchrony, a term used to describe the mismatch between the speeds of visual and auditory information processing activity in acts of literacy (Breznitz, 2008).

While the characteristics and traits of dyslexia continue to remain the subject of intensive research, they also reflect the understanding and observation of the professionals who have worked to help learners gain necessary literacy skills in formal, informal and domestic learning settings. For any new theory to have a strong case for being a unifying theory of dyslexia, it would have to satisfy all the known characteristics and qualities of dyslexia, but it would need also to provide guidance for practitioners. It would not only have to account for the key theories, including genetic and neuroscientific findings, but also provide an explanation of why the approaches and interventions known to be useful in teaching and learning for pupils and students who experience dyslexia are effective. These would include not only specialist interventions, but also those elements encompassed by the dyslexia-friendly approach.

Dyslexia and other difficulties

Often there are overlapping difficulties between dyslexia and other learning characteristics. Dyscalculia and Developmental Coordination Disorder (DCD), also known as dyspraxia, have been discussed in Chapter 5, but other individual learning characteristics may include autism or Asperger's syndrome (Autistic Spectrum conditions), attentional difficulties with or without hyperactivity (Attention Deficit Hyperactivity Disorder) and Specific Language Difficulties. Emotional and Behavioural Difficulties may also be included in an understanding of specific learning difficulties.

Increasing numbers of learners are entering FE and HE with diagnoses describing an Autistic Spectrum condition; more frequently this will be Asperger's Syndrome, with its association of high levels of intellectual capacity and functioning. Students will be overcoming difficulties with social communication, therefore small talk or conversation can be problematic. Social interaction, which can affect group work, may be compromised and being able to use imagination may be difficult, with learners preferring to follow a single train of thought or concept. This is a capacity which should not be seen as necessarily negative, since it may make learners the lead experts in their field.

Changes to timetables or the routine of the learning environment will create anxieties for students with these types of difficulties. Behaviours resulting from the kind of strong interest and involvement, and at times single-mindedness, associated with Asperger's syndrome may make examinations or assignment deadlines particularly stressful. It is helpful for the college or university to support learners by ensuring that they have someone who is a point of contact to help deal with issues that arise. It may also help to have an area that students can go to so that they can have 'time out' if stressed.

A 'colour conversation chart' has been developed by Gray (2008) for use with young learners experiencing ASC to aid them in communicating when they are angry or upset, but are not able to fully discuss the issues. A progress/personal tutor could use this as a way of explaining issues in class and to help identify why certain behaviours might cause stressful incidents; for example, between a student and his or her peers, and also between a student and his or her teachers, tutors and lecturers.

Dyslexia-friendly practices, when students experience co-occurring difficulties, include methods and materials that support organisation and memory, writing difficulties and the understanding of reading material for the course. In addition, some students experience sensitivity to their environment with regard to features such as noise, fluorescent lights and temperature, responding with a level of distress that is hard to comprehend for someone who does not experience it themselves. Attention to these factors in the learning setting can help students to get most benefit from their study experiences. This can be aided by enabling them to access their classroom before the rest of the group arrives, in order to be able to settle down and focus. There may also be a preference to sit in the same seat and to use the same computer; and if the learning setting is busy, the provision of a regular, visually and aurally quiet, personal study area would be helpful.

To maintain a course of study, students have to be able to organise their routines to arrive on time to classes, with the necessary materials and equipment required for that day. They will be processing a lot of new information presented in a number of formats – handouts, SMART board presentations, sequencing and understanding tasks to be carried out in a practical activity, taking notes while listening to the tutor – these are just some examples of the challenges faced by learners experiencing a specific learning difficulty. Within dyslexia itself there may be different emphases upon visual processing, auditory processing, phonological processing, memory, speed of processing or organisation.

When assessing access arrangements it is important to ensure that learners are happy with the recommendations. It may be necessary to arrange for learners with dyslexia to have their own room for an examination because a large, busy examination hall can be distracting and create anxiety. Teaching staff should be aware of the 'carrier' language being used in class as there may be difficulties with semantic processing. They will need to ensure that there is an opportunity to check understanding of the topic and essay briefs. Support staff can guide learners by using a graphic organiser or writing frame.

Transition is particularly important for students with co-occurring difficulties, as change can create anxieties, whether it is from school to college or college to university. It will benefit incoming students to visit the new campus, become familiar with the surroundings and travel arrangements that will have to be made to access the site. A move from college to university can be particularly fraught with the greater focus on independent learning, in addition to the environment change from a classroom to a large lecture hall. It would also be helpful to be able to experience how study takes place in the learning setting prior to joining, so that any learning needs can be addressed by the disability coordinator, if necessary highlighting the importance of note-taking skills and possibly arranging a 'buddy' or mentor to be a support contact. An assessment for Disabled Students' Allowance will be essential to fund a support package.

A study by Everatt, Weeks and Brooks (2008) looked at the difficulties experienced by different SEN groups including students with dyslexia, dyspraxia and attention deficit disorders. They found that all groups showed evidence of literacy difficulties but there were different reasons for their difficulties in acquiring literacy skills. It may be that rather than providing labels, which is necessary for funding purposes, it would be better to highlight the importance of a range of assessments that should be carried out to determine a profile of strengths and weaknesses that in turn will inform an appropriate support package for a new student.

Experiencing attention deficit and hyperactivity disorder (ADHD or ADD) is likely to prevent a student from maintaining focus. He or she may be restless or behave impulsively. Students with difficulties like these will require clear guidelines of behaviour, and may need to understand that there is a minimum level of behaviour that is expected in the college or university environment and what is the nature of this. Negotiation is essential and time should be taken to deal with the reasons for inappropriate behaviour – not when students or teachers, tutors or lecturers are in a state of heightened emotion; this will not resolve any issues.

Ghelani et al. (2004) examined reading difficulties in adolescents with ADHD. They found that there was a slower reading rate; therefore when presented with large amounts of text, the ability of students to maintain their attention and to be able to fully comprehend the content will be challenged. This difficulty, compounded with dyslexia, exacerbates literacy difficulties and is likely to require sensitivity and dyslexia-friendly methods and materials in the quest for successful outcomes.

Neurodiversity

Greater understanding gained through neuroscience has brought a realisation that just as areas within the brain do not have firm boundaries, but overlap in with each other, so too the dimensions of dyslexia have 'fuzzy' boundaries. The consideration of overlap with other learning characteristics or with other dyslexia characteristics, is an increasingly important area for dyslexia discourse.

'Neurodiversity' is a term which recognises that developmental diversity is an aspect of human development and that neurodiverse individuals have certain difficulties in common as opposed to the majority of the population who may be termed neurotypical. The word 'neurodiversity' emphasises the social model of disability and does not have the negative aspect of the commonly-used term 'co-morbidity'. Frequent difficulties for people who might consider themselves within this group include organisation, memory, concentration and sequencing. The Developmental Adult Neuro-Diversity Association (DANDA) has a useful website that includes a diagram, 'The make-up of neurodiversity' showing neurodiverse characteristics and their overlap. This can be found at www.danda.org.uk/pages/neuro-diversity.php

Students with dyslexia and another SpLD may categorise themselves on the UCAS form as having 'multiple', 'hidden' or 'other' disabilities. However, the impact of experiencing more than one disability may be more than an 'additive' value but more of a 'logarithmic' or cumulative increase of difficulty in studying and coping with everyday life. Griffin and Pollack's (2009) description of the experience of 27 current and past university students, notes how students viewed their disability either as a 'difference' or as a 'medical deficit'. The former has a positive connotation, while the latter is a more functional label associated with application for DSA funding and support.

Visual stress, scotopic sensitivity, Meares-Irlen Syndrome

Meares-Irlen Syndrome (MIS) (identified by Meares in New Zealand and Irlen in the US independently, but at roughly the same time in the 1980s) is experienced as visual stress or visual instability in which black text on a white background appears distorted. The distortion varies and can be experienced as, for example, letters moving, words being too close together or only one portion of the page being in focus. Students with MIS find they cannot read for long periods, sometimes for no longer than 20 minutes without having a headache or migraine. Research into the cause or causes of MIS has provided no concrete answers. A magnocellular deficit (magnocells, situated in the lateral geniculate nucleus [LGN], are concerned with visual motion perception) has been suggested (Stein, 2003) but is not conclusive. No clear reason can be given why coloured overlays should ameliorate or remove visual stress, although a redistribution of cortical hyperexcitability has been suggested (Wilkins, 2003).

Some students may have been assessed for coloured overlays before admission to university but some students, even mature students, can arrive at college or university without realising they have a recognised difficulty. Indeed they often find it hard to understand the question, 'How does black print on white paper look to you?'. An assessment involves a comparison of different coloured overlays and a reading rate test. Often the reaction to an overlay placed on top of black text on white paper can be dramatic as words that formerly moved become stationary and the student can read with ease. Changing the background colour can remove or at least minimise the discomfort, and increase the reading rate. Coloured overlays, coloured eye-level rulers, coloured lenses, printing/writing on coloured paper or changing the background colour of a computer screen can enable students to read with relative ease.

The debate: is dyslexia a disability?

As Chapter 8 suggests, the concept of whether dyslexia is a viewed as a disability depends to some extend on where a person lives. In some countries it is not recognised at all, in others it is accepted that some people will experience a considerable and specific difficulty in gaining literacy skills. Sometimes the idea of a specific learning difficulty is subsumed within a general wish to support learners who are underachieving. In other settings, recognition might be on the basis of a different terminology. Consequently, to speak of dyslexia sometimes means a possible confrontation with a different argument, one where the term 'dyslexia' is not used, and that the characteristics of dyslexia are therefore felt to be unacknowledged and avoided, possibly for resourcing reasons.

However, in the UK the Codes of Practice recognise the position of dyslexia and its identity as a disability in relation to the 1995 DDA. This act, when seeking to consider whether impairment should be considered as a disability, employs the criteria of severity to the point of affecting everyday living, together with the long-standing nature of the impairment. All other considerations of whether or not dyslexia is a disability are subject to these criteria. Since dyslexia is experienced within a range of difficulty, for some people it will be disabling.

Key technique: change the colour of the computer screen

For learners who experience discomfort from the effect of black print on a white ground, a way of ameliorating this effect is to change the background colour of the screen when writing or reading a document. This can also be effective for people who do not generally consider that they experience visual stress; eye muscles may be felt to relax when background colour is changed from white to a pastel shade. In Microsoft Word for Windows this can be done by following the menu trail of: Word (program); format; background and then carry out the colour change to suit preference. In Microsoft Vista the route is Word (program); page layout; page background; page color (colour) and then carry out the colour change. In Microsoft Word 2004 for Mac, Version 11.3, the menu trail is: format; background. This opens a window which enables the background colour to be changed. In 'finder', the background colour of windows can be set using: view: show view options, but the colour shows in icon view only.

Other application software will have different methods. For example, in Excel, the background colour of the cells can be changed by using 'cell styles' or by selecting cells and using 'format painter'.

What does the Code of Practice say about diversity of disability?

Part 4 of the *Disability Discrimination Act 1995: Code of Practice Post-16* recognises the diversity and range of disability, together with the impact of preconceptions in creating barriers. The Code warns against making assumptions about how people's disabilities will affect them, acknowledging that individuals experience their disabilities in different ways. Hidden impairments are also covered, 'for example, mental illness or mental health conditions, learning disabilities, dyslexia, diabetes and epilepsy' (DRC, 2007: 32, para. 3.3). The duty is always to avoid discrimination by making necessary adjustments, and to ensure that this happens, the Code recommends seeking the views of people with disabilities themselves.

Case study: Grace; experiencing co-occurring learning needs

Grace, aged 25, was following a course of higher level study in computer science. She had her DSA already in place, which identified learning needs in the areas of Asperger's syndrome, ADD and dyslexia. In spite of her difficulties, her overall level of ability was clear to all. Grace's parent had contacted the institution in advance and as a result early contact was made with the Connexions service. This enabled a transition programme to be planned that would put support in place as soon as Grace became an official student.

Grace was invited to visit the department to familiarise herself with arrangements in advance of beginning study. A particular work area was designated for her, providing both consistency and lack of visual distraction. Provision made for her included a note-taker, mentor/support worker, specialist tuition and assistive software. However, Grace did not always attend lectures when she thought that she already knew enough about their content.

The FE specialist comments

The issue of attendance would be important in FE as this would affect course targets for attendance and retention. If Grace was showing that assignments were being completed on time and demonstrating understanding then there may be the opportunity to make a special arrangement for her. This would need to be discussed with Grace and her parent. The role of the mentor would be important in ensuring the link between Grace and the college is maintained. The learning support coordinator would also play an important role by regular reviews to ensure Grace's needs were being met and that she was on target to complete her qualification.

The HE specialist comments

The support that Grace needs to be successful at university takes time to implement so having her DSA in place is a good start. The specialist tutor needs to be flexible when working with Grace, particularly if there are issues of time management or if Grace wants to attend only when she has specific questions, but, if so, the tutor could liaise with the mentor to help Grace attend her appointments. In helping Grace to analyse questions a graphical representation of the problem, along with a specialist dictionary, could be used. When working on her final project, it would be good to alert Grace and her mentor to come for sessions at the planning stage of her write-up as this will make for an easier process. Grace may find it difficult to include the intermediate steps in any aims or goals of the project and it will be necessary to elicit these from her. In addition, sessions may involve bringing her back to the main target of the appointment as her ADD may make her mind stray from the work in hand. The tutor should allow her a certain amount of leeway in this case but gently draw her back to focus on her write-up.

∿ Points for discussion

- Should Grace's non-attendance give cause for concern?
- Is it appropriate for her mentor to encourage Grace to come out of her individual work area and mingle?
- How can the teacher, tutor or lecturer help Grace approach the demands of her final year project?
- Are there any circumstances in which it would be appropriate to contact Grace's parent during her studies?

Since Grace did not always attend lectures, questions of due diligence were raised, but it was clear that she was responding well to the challenge of study and was on course to achieve a good outcome. The complex nature of the subject presented real challenges for the support staff but by dint of their own hard study they were able to keep pace with the student's needs. Dyslexia impacted upon her study only when she needed to write up her work for her final project and when she needed help to analyse questions because she was likely to take them too literally.

Summary

1 The theorisation of dyslexia is a continuing project, currently changing in line with new information from brain scanning, genetic research and evidence from other languages and orthographies. In addition to long-standing interests in the phonological, magnocellular and cerebellar accounts of dyslexia, there is a renewed interest in connectedness, speed of processing, attention and memory.

2 A second current trend is the focus on neurodiversity and overlapping characteristics that include, and impact upon, dyslexia. The neurodiversity perspective includes a move away from a deficit-based view.

3 Although Meares-Irlen syndrome has been debated since its introduction in the 1980s, it seems to be the case that some learners are affected by black print on a white background, and can be helped by the use of tinted papers, tinted lenses or coloured overlays. For some people this experience will overlap with dyslexia.

Further reading

Channock, K. (2007) 'How do we not communicate about dyslexia? – the discourse that distances scientists, disabilities staff, all advisers, students and lecturers from one another', *Journal of Academic Language and Learning*, 1(1): A33–A43.

Jamieson, J. and Jamieson, C. (2004) *Managing Asperger's Syndrome at College and University: A Resource for Students, Tutors and Support Services.* London: David Fulton.

Kriss, I. and Evans, B.J.W. (2005) 'The relationship between dyslexia and Meares-Irlen syndrome', *Journal of Research in Reading,* 28: 350–64.

Assistive software

The software used in the graphical representation at the start of this chapter is Spark-Space and is available from www.barrybennett.co.uk/software/mindmapping/sparkspace.php

Student comment

'You're painfully aware that there are people who are researchers in their area but don't hold teaching qualifications – that isn't to say that they were all not understanding … but it definitely helped that they'd been told I was dyslexic; it made a world of difference. I had a good student experience – I had it on a level playing field, which made me feel that if I put my back into it, I could really do well'. Chris

Appendix 1   List of acronyms

ADD	Attention Deficit Disorder
ADHD	Attention Deficit Hyperactivity Disorder
ADSHE	Association of Dyslexia Specialists in Higher Education
AHEAD	Association on Higher Education and Disability (North America)
ALG	Adult Learning Grant
ALS	Additional Learner Support
AMA	Advanced Modern Apprenticeship
ASC	Autistic Spectrum Conditions (e.g. Autism/Asperger's Syndrome)
ASL	American Sign Language
BDA	British Dyslexia Association
BPS	British Psychological Society
CAO	Central Applications Office
CILIP	Chartered Institute of Library and Information Professionals
CoP	Code of Practice
CoVE	Centre of Vocational Excellence
CPD	Continuous Professional Development
DANDA	Developmental Adult Neuro-Diversity Association
DCD	Developmental Coordination Disorder (also known as dyspraxia)
DCSF	Department for Children, Schools and Families
DDA	Disability Discrimination Act
DDP	Diploma Development Partnerships
DEL	Department for Employment and Learning
DES	Department of Education and Science
DfES	Department for Education and Skills
DoE	Department of Education
DRC	Disability Rights Commission
DSA	Disabled Students' Allowance
DTLLS	Diploma in Teaching in the Lifelong Learning Sector
EBD	Emotional and Behavioural Difficulties
ESF	European Social Fund
FCF	Financial Contingency Fund
FE	further education
HE	higher education
HEA	Higher Education Act
HMIE	Her Majesty's Inspectorate of Education
HND	Higher National Diploma
IA	Initial Assessment
ICT	information and communications technology

IDA	International Dyslexia Association
IEP	individual education plan
IFL	Institute for Learning
ILP	Individual Learning Plan
ISHEDS	Identification and Support in Higher Education for Dyslexic Students
L2	Second language
LA	Local Authority
LD	Learning Disability
LDD	Learning Disabilities and/or Difficulties
LGN	Lateral Geniculate Nucleus
LSA	Learner Support Agreement
LSC	Learning and Skills Council
MIS	Meares-Irlen Syndrome
NVQ	National Vocational Qualifications
Ofsted	Office for Standards in Education
Patoss	The Professional Association of Teachers of Students with Specific Learning Difficulties
QAA	Quality Assurance Agency for Higher Education
SEN	Special Educational Needs
SENCO	Special Educational Needs Coordinator
SENDA	Special Educational Needs and Disability Act
SENCoP	Special Educational Needs Code of Practice
SENDO	Special Educational Needs and Disability Order
SpLD	Specific Learning Difficulty
STEM	Science, Technology, Engineering and Mathematics
UCAS	Universities and Colleges Admissions Service
UID	Universal Instructional Design
WBL	Work-Based Learning (refers to NVQ programmes)
WRIT	Wide Range Intelligence Test
WRL	Work-Related Learning (refers to 14–16 provision)

Appendix 2   Self-evaluation/audit tool

Part 1: the dyslexia-friendly lecture room   **Date:** ....

A) Text resources available in the classroom/study room/lecture theatre	Never	Sometimes (less than 50 per cent)	Middling (about 50 per cent)	Usually (more than 50 per cent)	Always
1 Font is clearly distinguishable, with rounded shape, and two-story 'a', e.g. 'Ariel'.					
2 Photocopies are clean and clear.					
3 Text is in small groups: five lines maximum if possible.					
4 There are frequent subheadings, shown in bold.					
5 Off-white or tinted paper is used.					
6 Blocks of text are clearly separated.					
7 Headings/subheadings are clearly separated from text.					
8 Diagrams and illustrations are used.					
9 Diagrams and illustrations give same information as, or relate to, text.					
10 Diagrams and illustrations are near relevant text.					
11 Texts are given ahead of time for practice purposes.					
Total					

(Continued)

Appendix 2   (Continued)

B) Room arrangements	Never	Sometimes (less than 50 per cent)	Middling (about 50 per cent)	Usually (more than 50 per cent)	Always
1 Care is taken so that learners with possible dyslexia see and hear the lecturer clearly.					
2 Learners experiencing possible dyslexia have opportunities to work with their peers.					
3 Learners experiencing possible dyslexia have opportunities to work in a quiet area.					
4 Learners experiencing possible dyslexia have opportunities to display their understanding.					
5 Visual displays conform to text resource guidelines (see A above).					
6 Learners who request tinted paper may have it.					
Total					

C) Affective aspects	Never	Sometimes (less than 50 per cent)	Middling (about 50 per cent)	Usually (more than 50 per cent)	Always
1 Practitioners know and use learners' preferred individual learning styles (particularly visual, auditory or kinaesthetic).					
2 Practitioners challenge learners to use different learning styles in a manageable way.					
3 Practitioners know their own preferred individual learning styles (their comfort zone).					
4 Practitioners challenge themselves to move outside their own comfort zone.					
5 Judgements of laziness are avoided.					
6 Learners' reading in front of class is voluntary (rather than by adult selection).					
7 Learners' writing on the board or in front of class is voluntary.					
8 Rewards can be achieved by all the learners in the group.					
9 Learning tasks consider and deal with emotional issues first.					
10 Care is taken that learners are not teased for literacy difficulties.					
11 Care is taken to protect learners' feelings.					
Total					

(Continued)

Appendix 2 (Continued)

D) Room interactions	Never	Sometimes (less than 50 per cent)	Middling (about 50 per cent)	Usually (more than 50 per cent)	Always
1 Learners' concerns about their own literacy are respected.					
2 Use of a loud, raised voice by the practitioner is avoided (it destroys thinking).					
3 Lecturers liaise with dyslexia specialist(s).					
4 Ranking of learners according to their literacy skills is avoided.					
5 Attendance of learners experiencing possible or actual dyslexia is high.					
6 There is a marking policy in use that does not penalise dyslexia significantly.					
7 There is a dyslexia policy in place.					
8 Lecturers are familiar with the dyslexia policy.					
Total					

E) General dyslexia-friendly teaching and learning	Never	Sometimes (less than 50 per cent)	Middling (about 50 per cent)	Usually (more than 50 per cent)	Always
Teaching					
1 Instructions are clearly identified on the page or board.					
2 Statements are clear, without ambiguity (check with another person).					
3 Explanations are repeated, in different ways, as required by the learners.					
4 Timescale of a task is clearly stated, supportively (see statement 5 below).					
5 Extra time is allowed for learners to finish written work if necessary.					
6 Length of product (how much you want the learners to do) is clearly stated.					
7 Subject-specific words are linked to clear concepts.					
8 Practitioner talking is reduced (maximum 10 minutes).					
9 Board copying is reduced (maximum five lines).					
10 Handouts are available to reduce board copying (following guidelines in A above).					
11 Input is given in small chunks.					
12 Input takes account of multisensory learning – visual, auditory, kinaesthetic.					
13 VAK stimuli and tasks are close together.					
14 Teaching uses diagrams and illustrations.					

(Continued)

Appendix 2   (Continued)

	Never	Sometimes (less than 50 per cent)	Middling (about 50 per cent)	Usually (more than 50 per cent)	Always
15 Teaching uses bullet points and lists.					
16 Colour is used as an identifier: colour coding, highlighting, colour blocks for focus.					
17 New concepts are linked to previous concepts.					
18 New techniques are linked to previous techniques.					
19 Changes acknowledge what learners say about how best they learn.					
20 Assessment/marking criteria are clearly stated, including those for alternative formats.					
Learning					
21 Learners' output uses diagrams and illustrations.					
22 Learners' output uses bullet points and numbered lists.					
23 Learners can use alternative means of recording, e.g. poster, tape, ICT.					
24 Learners are asked how best they learn.					
25 Learners are allowed to ask questions.					
26 Learners' output is judged predominantly on quality and content.					
Total					

Self-evaluation/audit tool
Part 2: the departmental self-evaluation process

To conclude the departmental self-evaluation process answer the following questions:

1 Which do you think are the most important out of all the self-evaluation items?
....
....
....

2 How do you think your department's lecturing practice is doing in relation to those items? What are the strengths and weaknesses of the department's lecturing practice?
....
....
....

3 As a result of undertaking this self-evaluation, what three priority targets would you now set for the coming year (or shorter period)?
1 ....
2 ....
3 ....

4 Are there any further comments or reminders for when you look back on this evaluation?
....
....
....

Date of this evaluation:..................   Date of next evaluation:................
Evaluation carried out by:..

Dyslexia-Friendly Further and Higher Education © B. Pavey, M. Meehan and A. Waugh 2010

Appendix 3   Suggestions for a policy on dyslexia in FE/HE

1 Assessment of a SpLD

1.1 Dyslexia, a specific learning difficulty (SpLD), is a registered disability. Students who have a report by an educational psychologist or other appropriately qualified professional as evidence of a SpLD are eligible for appropriate support without compromising academic standards.

1.2 In further education, learners will be assessed in accordance with the Joint Council for Qualifications guidelines. A suitably qualified specialist teacher employed by the college, a qualified psychologist or LA specialist will complete a diagnostic report determining the presence of a SpLD and a Form 8 will be completed to confirm the adjustments required. This should indicate information relating to a history of need or a history of provision, and arrangements should reflect the learner's 'normal way of working'.

1.3 The assessments used will be appropriate and reflect the recommendations of the *SpLD Working Group 2005/DfES Guidelines* (July 2005) for assessments of SpLDs in higher education.

1.4 The assessment report will include recommendations for teaching and learning as well as access arrangements.

2 Legislation

2.1 The institution is required by law to support disabled students effectively. The Special Educational Needs and Disability Act (SENDA) 2001 being Part IV of the Disability Discrimination Act (DDA) 1995, states that the institution must:

   a) avoid discriminating against disabled students
   b) make reasonable adjustments to facilitate students' learning
   c) avoid creating unnecessary barriers to achievement, but not at the expense of academic standards
   d) be anticipatory; requiring departments to plan ahead for the needs of future students.

2.2 The Quality Assurance Agency (QAA) places specific expectations on institutions to provide disabled students with the same opportunities as their peers through its *Code of Practice for the Assurance of Academic Quality and Standards*.

2.3 In further education, the statutory regulation of external qualifications in England, Wales and Northern Ireland 2004 (para 9) states that awarding bodies must 'ensure access and equality of opportunity while safeguarding the integrity of the qualifications'.

3 Reasonable adjustments

3.1 SENDA (DfES, 2001) uses the term 'reasonable adjustment' as the measure by which provision for disabled students is set.

3.2 The term 'reasonable adjustment' is open to interpretation but it may be considered as: 'A necessary accommodation or alteration to existing academic programmes, offering individuals the opportunity to demonstrate their abilities' (Association of Dyslexia Specialists in Higher Education, ADSHE, 2007: 3, para. 2.2).

4 What is Dyslexia?

4.1 [Institutions may want to give their preferred definition of dyslexia here, for example the BDA or Dyslexia Action definition, followed by:

4.2 An explanation of how dyslexia is likely to affect students. For example, one of the aspects of dyslexia that affects literacy is a difficulty in associating sounds with pictures and is linked to relatively inefficient rapid information-processing capabilities and short-term memory. Consequently, dyslexic students experience difficulties in reading, writing, spelling and mathematics.]

5 Recording lectures

5.1 Recording lectures is considered a reasonable adjustment. Any recording is for private use only.

5.2 In the case of a tutorial or seminar where the information may be shared and of a confidential nature, agreement of all those present is required.

6 Assessment and examination provision

6.1 Fair assessment should be guaranteed for all students including those with particular assessment arrangements.

6.2 In FE qualifications where learners are not completing examinations but are expected to show evidence of competence determining a particular level of ability, this evidence of competence can be presented by using mechanical, electronic and other aids, as long as the aids are generally commercially available.

6.3 It is necessary to ensure that learners can meet the specified criteria and that adjustments reflect learners' normal ways of working.

6.4 All assessed work submitted by students is eligible for marking with reference to the institution's guidelines.

6.5 If the institution has a policy of anonymous marking, in order for the college or university to comply with the Special Educational Needs and Disability Act, students with SpLDs should have the opportunity to have their examination booklets and coursework endorsed. Their work may be identified by means of a stamp, sticker or other alternative according to the policy of the Institution.

6.6   It may not be possible for students with SpLDs to identify their work, for example in a foreign language test where the grammar, punctuation and spelling is being assessed. This must be publicised explicitly in the module handbook.

6.7   Extensions to deadlines should be considered but successive extensions may not help the student.

6.8   25 per cent extra time in examinations and class tests (including practical sessions) is commonly recommended by needs assessors and educational psychologists for students who have been assessed with SpLDs.

6.9   Needs assessors or educational psychologists may recommend other accommodations; for example, the use of a reader.

6.10   These recommendations should be adopted at the request of the student and after discussion with the disability office.

6.11   A reader or the use of screen-reading software cannot be provided where reading or understanding of written words is an element being assessed such as in Key Skills Communication. As an alternative it may be appropriate to offer extra time of 50 per cent.

6.12   A learner with ASC or EBD may require a rest break and a separate room for examination or assessment.

7 Marking coursework and examination scripts

7.1   Course assignments, when being marked, should reflect the knowledge demonstrated by a learner.

7.2   Learners should not be penalised for errors in punctuation, spelling and grammar.

8 Alternative forms of assessment

8.1   Alternative forms of assessment should be considered when at the design stage of a module.

8.2   In the case of professional examinations or where accuracy in written language is essential alternative forms of assessment may not be an option.

8.3   Students should be involved in discussions concerned with an alternative assessment format.

8.4   If it is not possible to make any adjustment, it must be clear on what grounds this decision has been made.

8.5   If a student is assessed as having a SpLD during the course of an academic year and his or her marks are at the borderline for passing a module, re-marking completed coursework within that year should be considered, where practicable.

Appendix 4 Template plan for writing essays

This works for anything that does not already provide a specific format, e.g. essays, dissertations, theses, business plans, reports, papers, books.

Useful techniques:
1 Background → present position → way forward
2 Tell them what you're going to tell them → tell them → tell them what you told them.

Introduction
(Tell the reader what you are going to tell them)
What is the subject?
Why is it important?
Why is it important to you?
Where does it start?
How is it structured?
Where does it end?

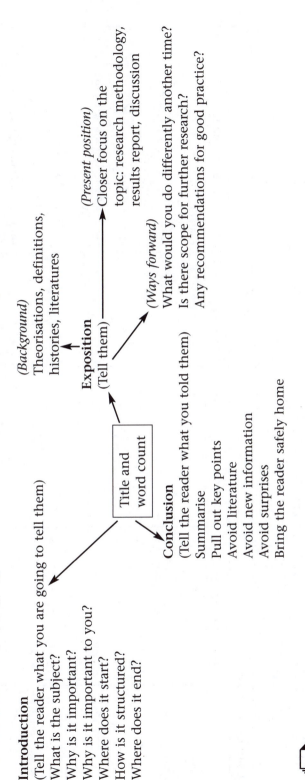

Title and word count

(Background)
Theorisations, definitions, histories, literatures

Exposition
(Tell them)

(Ways forward)
What would you do differently another time?
Is there scope for further research?
Any recommendations for good practice?

(Present position)
Closer focus on the topic: research methodology, results report, discussion

Conclusion
(Tell the reader what you told them)
Summarise
Pull out key points
Avoid literature
Avoid new information
Avoid surprises
Bring the reader safely home

Dyslexia-Friendly Further and Higher Education © B. Pavey, M. Meehan and A. Waugh 2010

Appendix 5   Lecture plan

Learning Outcomes:

Time	Teacher activity	Learner activity	Resources	Dyslexia access reminders
				Visual input
				Aural input
				Kinaesthetic input
				All these close together
				Materials checked for being dyslexia-friendly
				Short spelling list
				Scaffolded writing
				Minimum board copying
				Use of diagrams, charts
				Small work chunks
				Individual targets

		Recapitulation
		Opportunities for: • extra time • working with peers • showing knowledge • pupil/student ICT use

<u>Access arrangements for individual students</u>

<u>Assessment of outcomes</u>

1 Knowledge and understanding (grasp of essential aspects).
2 Intellectual skills (positives, negatives, analysis; summaries, judgements, arguments, reasoning, synthesis, evaluation, logical connection, ordering).
3 Professional/practice skills (demonstrate principles and contexts in fields of study and employment context; wide range of sources, personal responsibility, decision-making, technology, relevant techniques and processes).
4 Transferable skills: communication, ICT, problem–solving, working with others, learning to learn.

Appendix 6   Useful websites

Association of Dyslexia Specialists in Higher Education: www.adshe.org.uk

Autism Research Centre: www.autismresearchcentre.com (Features the research and work of Professor Simon Baron-Cohen et al. There are useful research articles and information for educationalists and those involved with young people and adults with autistic spectrum and Asperger's syndrome difficulties.)

Beattie Resources for Inclusion in Technology and Education: www.BRITE.ac.uk (BRITE was set up in Scotland following the Beattie report into FE in Scotland. The website features a lot of good advice for teachers and students in further and higher education and also advice on assistive technology.)

British Dyslexia Association: www.bdadyslexia.org.uk (This is a registered charity committed to dyslexia-friendly teaching practices and providing information on dyslexia.)

The Chartered Institute of Library and Information Professionals: www.cilip.org.uk (Represents staff and management involved in library and information services.)

The Developmental Adult Neuro-diversity Association (DANDA): www.danda. org.uk

Diploma Support Programme: www.diploma-support.org (Supports the 14–19 diploma programme with advice for schools and parents.)

Dyslexia Action: www.dyslexia-action.org.uk (Provides assessment centres throughout the UK and is one of the organisations responsible for the licensing of practitioners to carry out DSA assessments.)

The Dyslexia and Dyscalculia Interest Group (DDIG): http://ddig.lboro.ac. uk/www_links.html

Dyslexia at College: www.dyslexia-college.com (A support site for students at college or university.)

The Dyslexia SpLD Trust: www.thedyslexia-spldtrust.org.uk (Was launched in March 2009 and is supported by the British Dyslexia Association, Dyslexia Action, Helen Arkell Dyslexia Centre and Patoss. This site is aimed at practitioners and as an information and awareness raising site by all of these organisations.)

Dyspraxia Foundation: www.dyspraxiafoundation.org.uk (Provides support for those who experience dyspraxia and their families as well as advice for professionals.)

The Institute for Learning: www.ifl.ac.uk (Monitors the registration and CPD of teaching staff in FE.)

JISC TechDis Service: www.techdis.ac.uk (Aims to support the education sector by providing advice and guidance on assistive technology that will support learners with disabilities.)

National Association for Special Educational Needs: www.nasen.org.uk (Supports young people with special educational needs and the professionals who work with them.)

Patoss: www.patoss-dyslexia.org (Responsible for monitoring professional teachers who provide assessment and support throughout the UK for those experiencing dyslexia. Also provides licensed practitioner status to those carrying out DSA assessments.)

Teaching and Development Agency for Schools: www.tda.gov.uk (Responsible for the training and development of the school workforce. Features advice and guidance for those who would like to enter the teaching profession and for those who are already in the profession.)

References

Ansari, D. and Karmiloff-Smith, A. (2002) 'Atypical trajectories of number development: a neuroconstructivist perspective', *TRENDS in Cognitive Sciences*, 6 (12): 511–16.

Association of Dyslexia Specialists in Higher Education, (ADSHE) (2007) *Reasonable Adjustments in Academic Departments*, Borehamwood: ADSHE. Available online at: http://www.adshe.org.uk/wp-content/uploads/reasonableadjustments11.pdf

Association of Dyslexia Specialists in Higher Education, (ADSHE) (2007) *University Policy on Specific Learning Difficulties (Dyslexia)*. Borehamwood: The Disability Office, ADSHE.

Bartlett, D. and Moody, S. (2004) *Dyslexia in the Workplace*. London: Whurr.

Bloom, B.S. (1979) *Taxonomy of Educational Objectives. Book 1: Cognitive Domain*. London: Longman.

Breznitz, Z. (2008) 'The origin of dyslexia: the asynchrony phenomenon', in G. Reid, A. Fawcett, F. Manis and L. Seigel (eds), *The Sage Handbook of Dyslexia*. London: Sage.

British Dyslexia Association (n.d.) 'Dyslexia/inclusion friendly Quality Mark Initiative for further education institutions (sample document only)'. Available online at www.bdadyslexia.org.uk/downloads/sample%20standards.pdf

British Dyslexia Association (2006) 'Adult checklist'. Available online at www.bdadyslexia.org.uk/adultchecklistp.html

Brown, A. and Pollard, A. (eds) (2006) *14–19 Education and Training: A Commentary by the Teaching and Learning Research Programme*. London: TLRP, the Economic and Social Research Committee (ESRC).

Burden, B. (2008) 'Is dyslexia necessarily associated with negative feelings of self-worth? A review and implications for further research', *Dyslexia*, 14 (3): 188–96.

Burden, R. and Burdett, J. (2005) 'Factors associated with successful learning in pupils with dyslexia: a motivational analysis', *British Journal of Special Education*, 32 (2): 100–104.

Butterworth, B. (1999) *The Mathematical Brain*. London: Macmillan.

Butterworth, B. (2003) *Dyscalculia Screener*. London: NFER.

Butterworth, B. and Yeo, D. (2004) *Dyscalculia Guidance*. London: David Fulton.

Buzan, T. (2007) *The Buzan Study Skills Handbook*. London: BBC Active.

Castles, A. and Coltheart, M. (1993) 'Varieties of developmental dyslexia', *Cognition*, 47 (2): 149–80.

Center for Universal Design (1997) 'About Universal Design'. Available online at www.design.ncsu.edu/cud/about_ud/about_ud.htm

Channock, K. (2007) 'How do we not communicate about dyslexia? The discourse that distances scientists, disabilities staff, all advisers, students and lecturers from one another', *Journal of Academic Language and Learning*, 1 (1): A33–43.

Chartered Institute of Library and Information Professionals (CILIP) (2008) 'Self-assessment toolkit for learning resources services in further education colleges in England (a.k.a. 'English FE Toolkit'). Produced by the Colleges of Further and Higher Education Special Interest Group. Available online at: www.cilip.org.uk/specialinterestgroups/bysubject/cofhe/publications/fetoolkit.htm

Chasty, H. and Friel, J. (1991) *Children with Special Needs, Assessment Law and Practice: Caught in the Act*. London: Jessica Kingsley.

Chinn, S. (2003) 'Does dyscalculia add up?', *Dyslexia Review*, 14: 4–8.

Connelly, V., Campbell, S., MacLean, M. and Barnes, J. (2006) 'Contribution of lower order skills to the written composition of college students with and without dyslexia', *Developmental Neuropsychology*, 29 (1): 175–96.

Cooper, R. (2006) 'A social model of dyslexia', *Language Issues*, 18 (2): 24–26.

Dale, M. and Taylor, B. (2001) 'How adult learners make sense of their dyslexia', *Disability and Society*, 16 (7): 997–1008.

Dearing, R. (1996) *Review of Qualifications for 16–19 Year-Olds.* London: School Curriculum and Assessment Authority.

Department for Children, Schools and Families (DCSF) (2008) *The Work-Related Learning Guide.* London: DCSF. Available online at http://publications.teachernet.gov.uk

Department for Education and Skills (DfES) (2001) *Special Educational Needs Code of Practice.* Annesley: DfES Publications.

Department for Education and Skills (DfES) (2004) *A Framework for Understanding Dyslexia.* Annesley: DfES.

Department for Education and Skills (DfES) (2005) *The Specific Learning Difficulties Working Group 2005/DfES Guidelines.* London: HMSO.

Department for Education and Skills (DfES) (2006) *Further Education: Raising Skills, Improving Life Chances.* Annesley: DfES Publications.

Deponio, P. (2004) 'The co-occurrence of specific learning difficulties: implications for identification and assessment', in G. Reid and A. Fawcett (eds), *Dyslexia in Context, Research, Policy and Practice.* London: Whurr.

Disability Rights Commission (DRC) (2005) *The Duty to Promote Disability Equality.* London: TSO.

Disability Rights Commission (DRC) (2007) *Disability Discrimination Act 1995: Code of Practice Post-16.* London: TSO.

Dowker, A. (2004) 'Children's arithmetical difficulties' Sixth International Conference of the British Dyslexia Association, Warwickshire.

DuPre, L., Gilroy, D. and Miles, T. (2008) *Dyslexia at College* (third edition). London: Routledge.

Dyslexia Scotland (2006) 'What is dyslexia?' Available online at www.dyslexiascotland.org.uk/index.aspx?sid=5

Ecclestone, K. (2006) 'The future role of further education colleges', in A. Brown and A. Pollard (eds), *14–19 Education and Training: A Commentary by the Teaching and Learning Research Programme.* London: TLRP, the Economic and Social Research Committee (ESRC).

Everatt, J., Weeks, S. and Brookes, P. (2008) 'Profiles of strengths and weaknesses in dyslexia and other learning difficulties', *Dyslexia*, 14 (1): 16–41.

Facoetti, A., Lorusso, M., Paganoni, P., Cattaneo, C., Galli, R., Umilta, C. and Mascetti, G. (2003) 'Auditory and visual automatic attention deficits in developmental dyslexia', *Cognitive Brain Research*, 16 (2) (April): 185–91.

Fawcett, A. (2001) 'Recent research and development in dyslexia in relation to children of school age: a quarterly review for the Department for Education and Skills, the British Dyslexia Association and the Dyslexia Institute'. Review 1 September. Available online at www.whatdotheyknow.com/request/180/response/482/attach/5/Dyslexia

Fawcett, A . and Nicolson, R. (1998) *Dyslexia Adult Screening Test (DAST).* London: Pearson.

Fraser, V. and Zybutz, T. (2004) 'The dyslexia screening process in HE'. This paper is currently unavailable online. Further information about availability may be obtained from ADSHE (www.adshe.org.uk).

Frith, U. (1999) 'Paradoxes in the definition of dyslexia', *Dyslexia*, 5 (4): 192–214.

Fryer, R.H. (1997) 'Learning for the twenty-first century. First report of the National Advisory Group for continuing education and lifelong learning'. Available online at www.lifelonglearning.co.uk/nagccl/index.htm

Fuller, M., Healey, M., Bradley, A. and Hall, T. (2004) 'Barriers to learning: a systematic study of the experience of disabled students in one university', *Studies in Higher Education*, 29: 303–18.

General Medical Council (2008) '*Gateways to the professions. Advising Medical Students: encouraging disabled students*'. Available online at www.gmc-uk.org/education/undergraduate/undergraduate_policy/gateways_guidance/index.asp

Ghelani, K., Sidhu, R., Jain, U. and Tannock, R. (2004) 'Reading comprehension and reading related abilities in adolescents with reading disabilities', *Dyslexia*, 10 (4): 364–84.

Gilbride, N. (2007) *Research review report. Unpublished paper.* London: University of London.

Gilroy, D. (2004) 'Stress factors in the college student', in T. Miles (ed.) *Dyslexia and Stress.* London: Whurr.

Glutting, J., Adams, W. and Sheslow, D. (2000) *Wide Range Intelligence Test (WRIT)*. London: Pearson Assessment.

Goleman, D. (1995) *Emotional Intelligence.* London: Bloomsbury.

Gray, C. (2008) '*Comic strip conversation*'. Available online at www.abiq.org/2008%20Conference/Completed%20PDF%20handouts/GRAY-%20Comic%20Strip%20Conversations.pdf.

Griffin, E. and Pollak, D. (2009) 'Student experiences of neurodiversity in higher education: insights from the BRAINHE project', *Dyslexia*, 15 (1): 23–41.

Griffiths, Y. and Snowling, M. (2002) 'Predictors of exception word and non-word reading in dyslexic children: the severity hypothesis', *Journal of Educational Psychology*, 94 (1): 34–43.

Hall, T. and Healey, M. (2005) 'Disabled students' experiences of fieldwork', *Area*, 37 (4): 446–49.

Hargreaves, S. (2007) *Study Skills for Dyslexic Students.* London: Sage.

Harrison, A.G., Edwards, M.J. and Parker, K.C.H. (2008) 'Identifying students feigning dyslexia: preliminary findings and strategies for detection', *Dyslexia*, 14 (3): 228–46.

Her Majesty's Inspectorate of Education (HMIE) (2008) 'Education for learners with dyslexia'. Available online at www.hmie.gov.uk/documents/publication/eflwd.html

Her Majesty's Stationery Office (HMSO) (1995) *Disability Discrimination Act 1995*. London: HMSO.

Her Majesty's Stationery Office (HMSO) (2001) *Special Educational Needs and Disability Act.* London: HMSO.

Her Majesty's Stationery Office (HMSO) (2005) *Disability Discrimination Act 2005.* London: HMSO.

Hillier, Y. (2002) *Reflective Teaching in Further and Adult Education.* London: Continuum.

Honneth, A. (2004) 'Recognition and justice', *Acta Sociologica*, 47 (4): 351–64.

Irish Government (2000) *The Equal Status Act 2000.* Available online at www.irishstatutebook.ie/2000/en/ect/pub/0008/index.html

Jamieson, J. and Jamieson, C. (2004) *Managing Asperger's Syndrome at College and University: A Resource for Students, Tutors and Support Services.* London: David Fulton.

Jamieson, C. and Morgan, E. (2008) *Managing Dyslexia at University: A Resource for Students, Academic and Support Staff.* London: Routledge.

Kirby, A., Sugden, D., Beveridge, S., Edwards, L. and Edwards, R. (2008) 'Dyslexia and developmental co-ordination disorder in further and higher education: similarities and differences. Does the "label" influence the support given?', *Dyslexia*, 14 (3): 197–213.

Klassen, R., Neufeld, P. and Munro, F. (2005) 'When IQ is irrelevant to the definition of learning disabilities: Australian school psychologists' beliefs and practice', *Scholl Psychology International,* 26 (3): 297–316.

Kosc, L. (1974) 'Developmental dyscalculia', *Journal of Learning Disabilities*, 7: 159–62.

Kriss, I. and Evans, B.J.W. (2005) 'The relationship between dyslexia and Meares-Irlen syndrome', *Journal of Research in Reading*, 28 (3): 350–64.

Lawrence, D. (1985) 'Improving self-esteem and reading', *Educational Research*, 27 (3): 194–200.

Learning and Skills Council (LSC) and the Department for Education and Skills (DfES) (2007) *Delivering World Class Skills in a Demand-Led System*. Coventry: LSC.

Leitch, Lord, S. (2006) *Leitch Review of Skills: Prosperity for All in the Global Economy – World Class Skills. Final Report*. London: HMSO.

Lewis, B. (2002) 'Widening participation in higher education: the HEFCE perspective on policy and progress', *Higher Education Quarterly*, 56 (2): 204–19.

Long, R. (2009) *Intervention Toolbox: for Social, Emotional and Behavioural Difficulties*. London: Sage.

Martin, A. and McLoughlin, D. (2008) 'Employment experiences of adults with dyslexia'. Paper presented at the 2008 International Conference of the British Dyslexia Association, Harrogate.

Martin, D. and Pavey, B.E. (2008) *Presenting Your Research*. Handbook for Unit 5 of the Practitioner Inquiry in Education programme. Birmingham: School of Education, University of Birmingham.

McCrone, T., Wade, P. and Golden, S. (2007) *The Impact of 14–16-year-olds on Further Education Colleges*. Slough: NFER.

Meehan, M.M. (2008a) '*The experience of dyslexic students at university*'. Poster presented to Seventh International Conference of the British Dyslexia Association, Yorkshire.

Meehan, M.M. (2008b) '*Transitions in education*'. *Unpublished paper*. Swansea University.

Miles, T. (ed.) (2004) *Dyslexia and Stress*. London: Whurr.

Miller-Guron, L. and Lundberg, I. (2000) 'Dyslexia and second language reading: a second bite of the apple?', *Reading and Writing: An Interdisciplinary Journal*, 12: 41–61.

Mitchell, E. (2004) '*Following SENDA – institutional and individual responses to the needs of students with dyslexia*'. Paper presented to the Sixth International Conference of the British Dyslexia Association, Warwickshire.

Morton, J. and Frith, U. (1995) 'Causal modelling: a structural approach to developmental psychopathology', in D. Cicchetti and D.J. Cohen (eds) *Manual of Developmental Psychopathology*. New York: Wiley.

Nicholson, R. and Fawcett, A. (1999) 'Developmental dyslexia: the role of the cerebellum', *Dyslexia*, 5 (3): 155–71.

Nicholson, R. and Fawcett, A. (2008) *Dyslexia, Learning and the Brain*. London: Massachusetts Institute of Technology.

Orton, S.T. (1937) *Reading, Writing, and Speech Problems in Children*. New York: W.W. Norton.

Paracchini, S., Steer, C., Buckingham, L.L., Morris, A., Ring, S., Scerri, T., Stein, J., Pembrey, M., Ragoussis, J., Golding, J. and Monaco, A. (2008) 'Association of the KIAA0319 dyslexia susceptibility gene with reading skills in the general population', *American Journal of Psychiatry*, 165 (12): 1576–84.

Pavey, B.E. (2007) *The Dyslexia-Friendly Primary School*. London: Paul Chapman.

Peer, L. and Reid, G. (eds) (2000) *Multilingualism, Literacy and Dyslexia: A Challenge for Educators*. London: David Fulton.

Pico Educational Systems Ltd (2008) *The Home of QuickScan and StudyScan*. Available online at www.zyworld.com/studyscan

Pollak, D. (2005) *Dyslexia, the Self, and Higher Education*. Stoke on Trent: Trentham.

Price, G. (2006) 'Creative solutions to making technology work: three case studies of dyslexic writers in higher education', *ALT-J, Research in Learning Technology*, 14 (1): 21–38.

Price, G. and Skinner, J. (2007) *Support for Learning Differences in Higher Education: the Essential Practitioner's Manual*. Stoke on Trent: Trentham.

Quality Assurance Agency (QAA) (1999) *Code of Practice for the Assurance of Quality and Standards in Higher Education. Section 3: Students with Disabilities*. London: QAA.

Quality Assurance Agency (QAA) (2001) *Academic Infrastructure: The Framework for Higher Education Qualifications in England, Wales and Northern Ireland*. London: QAA.

Quality Assurance Agency (QAA) (2008) *The Framework for Higher Education Qualifications in England, Wales and Northern Ireland*. London: QAA.

Quality Assurance Agency (QAA) (2009) *Code of Practice for the Assurance of Quality and Standards in Higher Education. Section 3: Disabled Students*. Draft for consultation. London: QAA.

Rawls, J. (1971) *A Theory of Justice*. Harvard, MA: Harvard University Press.

Reid, A., Szczerbinski, M., Iskierka-Kasparek, E. and Hansen, P. (2008) 'Cognitive profiles of adult developmental dyslexics: theoretical implications', *Dyslexia*, 13: 1–24.

Reid, G., Fawcett, A., Manis, F. and Seigel, L. (eds) (2008) *The Sage Handbook of Dyslexia*. London: Sage.

Reid, G. and Kirk, J. (2001) *Dyslexia in Adults: Education and Employment*. Chichester: John Wiley & Sons.

Riddell, S., Wilson, A. and Tinklin, T. (2002) 'Disability and the wider access agenda: supporting disabled students in different institutional contexts', *Widening Participation and Lifelong Learning*, 4: 12–26.

Riddick, B. (1996) *Living with Dyslexia*. London: David Fulton.

Riddick, B., Farmer, M. and Sterling, C. (1997) *Students and Dyslexia: Growing up with a Specific Learning Difficulty*. London: Whurr.

Sanderson, A. (2000) 'Reflections on StudyScan', *Dyslexia*, 6: 284–90.

Scott, R. (2003) 'A counsellor's perspective on dyslexia', in M. Thomson (ed.) *Dyslexia Included*. London: David Fulton.

Shalev, R., Auerbach, J., Manor, O. and Gross-Tsur, V. (2000) 'Developmental dyscalculia: prevalence and prognosis', *European Child and Adolescent Psychiatry*, 9 (11): 58–64.

Singleton, C.H. (Chair) (1999) *'Dyslexia in higher education: policy, provision and practice'*. Report of the National Working Party on dyslexia in higher education. Hull: University of Hull on behalf of the Higher Education Funding Councils of England and Scotland.

Singleton, C.H. (2001) 'Computer-based assessment in education', *Educational and Child Psychology*, 18 (3): 58–74.

Singleton, C.H. (ed.) (2008) *Dyslexia Handbook 2008*. Bracknell: British Dyslexia Association.

Singleton, C.H., Horne, J.K. and Thomas, K.V. (2002) *Lucid Adult Dyslexia Screener (LADS)*. Beverley, East Yorkshire: Lucid Research Limited.

Smith, R. (2007) 'An overview of research on student support: helping students to achieve or achieving institutional targets? Nurture or de-nature?', *Teaching in Higher Education*, 12: 638–39.

Smythe, I. (2004) *'Dyslexia and English as an additional language'*. PowerPoint presentation. National Association of Disability Practitioners Spring Conference (March). PowerPoint presentation available at www.nadp-uk.org/events/spring2004.php

Smythe, I. (2005) Provision and use of Information Technology with Dyslexic Students in Universities in Europe, available online at http://www.welshdyslexia.info/minerva/book.pdf

Smythe, I. and Everatt, J. (2001) 'A new dyslexia checklist for adults in I. Smythe (ed) *The Dyslexia Handbook 2001*. Reading: British Dyslexia Association.

Smythe, I., Everatt, J. and Salter, R. (eds) (2004) *International Book of Dyslexia: A Cross-Language Comparison and Practice Guide*. Chichester: John Wiley & Sons.

Stein, J. (2001) 'The magnocellular theory of developmental dyslexia', *Dyslexia*, 7 (1): 12–36.

Stein, J. (2003) 'Visual motion sensitivity and reading', *Neuropsychologia*, 41: 1785–93.

Strunk, Jr, W. and White, E. (2000) *The Elements of Style* (fourth edition). London: Longman.

Sunderland, H., Klein, C., Savinson, R. and Partridge, T. (1997) *Dyslexia and the Bilingual Learner*. Stevenage: Avanti Books.

Taylor, C. (1994) 'The politics of recognition', in Gutmann, A. (ed.) *Multiculturalism: Examining the Politics of Recognition*. Princeton: Princeton University Press.

Trott, C. and Beacham, N. (2006) *'DyscalculiUM: a first-line screener for dyscalculia in higher education'*. Neurodiversity Conference, DeMontfort University, Leicester.

Trott, C. and Wright, F. (2003) 'Maths and dyslexia in further and higher education', in D. Pollack (ed.) *'Supporting the dyslexic student in HE and FE: strategies for success'*.

Proceedings of a one-day conference held at De Montfort University and the University of Hull (June).

Ullman, M. (2004) 'Contributions of memory circuits to language: the declarative/procedural model', *Cognition*, 92 (1–2): 213–70.

Wearmouth, J., Soler, J. and Reid, G. (2002) *Addressing Difficulties in Literacy Development*. London: RoutledgeFalmer.

Welsh Assembly Government (2002) *Special Educationl Needs Code of Practice for Wales*. Cardiff: Welsh Assembly Government.

Weschler, D. (1999) *Wechsler Adult Intelligence* Scale (third edition). Oxford: Pearson Assessment.

Wilkins, A. (2003) *Reading Through Colour: How Coloured Filters can Reduce Reading Difficulty, Eye Strain, and Headaches*. London: Wiley.

Willburger, E., Fussenegger, B., Moll, K., Wood, G., Landerl, K. (2008) 'Naming speed in dyslexia and dyscalculia', *Learning and Individual Differences*, 18 (2): 224–36.

Wolf, M. and Bowers, P. (1999) 'The double-deficit hypothesis for the developmental dyslexias', *Journal of Educational Psychology*, 91 (3): 415–38.

Yeo, D. (2003) *Dyslexia, Dyspraxia and Mathematics*. London: Whurr.

Zeff, R. (2007) 'Universal Design across the curriculum', *New Directions for Higher Education*, 137 (Spring): 27–44.

Ziegler, J. and Goswami, U. (2005) 'Reading acquisition, developmental dyslexia and skilled reading across languages: a psycholinguistic grain size theory', *Psychological Bulletin*, 131 (1): 3–29.

Ziegler, J., Perry, C., Ma-Wyatt, A., Ladner, D. and Schulte-Körne, G. (2003) 'Developmental dyslexia in different languages: language-specific or universal?', *Journal of Experimental Child Psychology*, 86 (3): 169–93.

Index